# LARCENY IN THE HEART

## THE ECONOMICS OF SATAN AND THE INFLATIONARY STATE

### ROUSAS JOHN RUSHDOONY

ROSS
HOUSE
BOOKS

VALLECITO, CALIFORNIA

Library of Congress Control Number: 2002095383
ISBN: 1-879998-32-7

*Printed in the United States of America*

**Our thanks to those who made
the 2002 reprinting of this book possible.**

Mr. & Mrs. Donald Alexander * Paul T. Bergaus * Clara Bianchi *
Michael & Marian Bowman * James & Judith Bruner *
John & Gloria Buzard * Dennis Clarys * Stephen & Janet Coakley *
Robert & Martha Coie * Kenneth W. Cope *
In Memory of Daniel Oliver Crews *
Richard & Elizabeth Crews * Jon & Patricia Davidson *
Dr. Anne L. Davis * David & Joan Dobert * Justin & Melanie Dock *
Dominion Covenant Church * Colonel & Miriam Doner *
In memory of Louise E. Duntz * John & Joan Dyer *
Rev. Dale Dykema & Reformation Presbyterian Church *
Dr. & Mrs. Nicholas H. Edwards * David & Maurietta Estler *
Harry & Marcella Fagan * Jack R. Faris * Robert & Marisa Frank *
Freedom Baptist Church *Michael & Mary Ann Frodella *
The Craig George Family * Dwight & Kathleen George *
Raphael A. Hanson III * Cathy Harnish * Keith & Antha Harnish *
Rev. & Mrs. Samuel D. Harrison * John William Helm *
William & Ruth Hewson * Dr. & Mrs. Herbert Hopper *
E.L.D.H. in memory of Lee & Thomas * Kenneth & Cindy Ii *
Earl & Dorothea Keener * Douglas Floyd Kelly * John B. King, Jr. *
David & Annie Knowles * Sarah Paris Kraft * Dr. & Mrs. Gary Kunsman *
John & Karen La Fear * Marguerite A. Lane * Dr. & Mrs. J.H. Lawson *
Gary Livingston * In memory of Muril & Florence Lovelace *
Joanna, Rachel & Daniel Manesajian * Steve & Belle Merritt *
Norman Milbank * Clint & Elizabeth Miller * Charles & Alfreida Moore *
Dr. Dean Moore * Timothy Patrick Murray * The Jim Nelson Family *
Dr. Heriberto Ortega * Chris & Anne Passerello *
The Howard Phillips Family * Gavin & Rachel Quill *
Greg Reger & Family * Steven Rogers * Frederic Rothfus *
Levi A. R. Rouse * Rebecca, Jill & Emily Rouse * April Rushdoony *
Terry & Janie Saxon * Virginia Schlueter * Anthony Schwartz *
Ford & Andrea Schwartz * Martin & Darlene Selbrede *
Guy Shea * Keith Shepherd *
SonRise Christian Community Church & Academy *
Phil & Petiflor Speilman * Eileen Stanley * Elmer & Naomi Stolzfus *
Martin Stroub * Scot Sullivan * Steve & Jacque Tanner *
Dr. David & Dorothy Terhune * Don & Betty Thompson *
Harry & Jo Ellen Valentine * Ellen Van Buskirk * Ellen Vasbinder *
Magnus Verbrugge * The Howard Walter Family *
Billie Welch * The Jeff White Family * Allan & Margaret Withington *
Roy S. Wright * David E. Young * Jeff & Cynthia Zylstra

Other books by
Rousas John Rushdoony


*The Institutes of Biblical Law, Vol. I*
*The Institutes of Biblical Law, Vol. II, Law & Society*
*The Institutes of Biblical Law, Vol. III, The Intent of the Law*
*Systematic Theology (2 volumes)*
*Hebrews, James & Jude*
*The Gospel of John*
*Romans & Galatians*
*Thy Kingdom Come*
*Foundations of Social Order*
*The "Atheism" of the Early Church*
*The Biblical Philosophy of History*
*The Mythology of Science*
*This Independent Republic*
*The Nature of the American System*
*Intellectual Schizophrenia*
*The Death of Meaning*
*The Word of Flux*
*The Messianic Character of American Education*
*The Philosophy of the Christian Curriculum*
*Christianity and the State*
*Salvation and Godly Rule*
*God's Plan for Victory*
*Politics of Guilt and Pity*
*Roots of Reconstruction*
*The One and the Many*
*Revolt Against Maturity*
*By What Standard?*
*Law & Liberty*

For a complete listing of available books
by Rousas John Rushdoony and other
Christian reconstructionists, contact:

**ROSS HOUSE BOOKS**
PO Box 67
Vallecito, CA 95251
www.rosshousebooks.org

# Table of Contents

# Part Two

# Part Three

# Introduction

One of the encouraging facts of our time is the rise of many able economists who are calling attention to the economic follies of our time. These are men of the Austrian school in the main. My debt to them is very great. I first learned the facts of sound money from Dr. Elgin Groseclose, then on economics in general from Dr. Hans Sennholz, and, by no means least of all, from my son-in-law, Dr. Gary North. The writings of many men, such as Von Mises, Röpke, Hazlitt, Greaves, Reisman, and many, many more have taught me much. We have today some excellent work done by The Foundation for Christian Economics (Gary North), The Foundation for Economic Education (Leonard Read), and The Institute for Monetary Research (Elgin Groseclose), to name but a few. Excellent economic reporting by newsletters also marks our day: Gary North's *Remnant Review*, R.E. McMaster's *The Reaper*, *The International Harry Schultz Letter*, and more. *Why then this book, by an "outsider," a theologian?*

Inflation is only in part and on the surface an economic problem. It is at heart a religious and moral problem. This is the fact that men avoid recognizing. Bernie Ward, writing on "The Psychology of Gold" in *Sky Magazine*, June, 1980 (The

Delta Air Lines in-flight magazine), sought to explain the use of gold in Freudian terms. Man's "need" for gold was explained away in terms of man's supposed immaturity and need for symbolic crutches. Not for a moment did Ward give consideration to economic factors. This should not surprise us. Modern man wants no factor external to himself to determine any facet of his life. Because man is determined to play god, he will not recognize any law order external to himself which can govern his way of life and impose limitations upon his fiat powers.

Our world economy is today bankrupt, because the world is morally and religiously bankrupt. We cannot restore our economic order without first of all restoring moral order. It has been often stated that inflation is larceny, but it is larceny not only by the central civil government or state but by every man. Because man has larceny in his heart, he creates an inflationary economy, i.e., he legalizes his will to steal. The corruption of money is a means of sinning legally, and men want nothing more then to sin legally and to call it virtue, or prosperity, or some like term. Economists are not lacking to say that it is so. The world has always been a good market for prostitutes, and a poor one for truth. However, because the world is God's creation and law order, it is the truth which in time shall prevail and triumph.

Rousas John Rushdoony<br>
Chalcedon<br>
Vallecito, California

*Note*:

Thanks are very, very much in order to Mr. Martin Selbrede, who donated his services to set type for this book (and also for Dr. Edward Murphy's *In Your Justice*) for Ross House Books. Mr. Selbrede's understanding of, faith in, and concern for the cause of Christian reconstruction is a joy to me.

The chapters on "Economics and the Doctrine of Man," and "The Polytheism of the Modern Mind: Political and Economic Heresies in the Modern Age," were prepared for and delivered to the Economic Institute for Research and Education (1005 12th Street, Boulder, Colorado 80302); the former was published by EIRE under that title. I am grateful to Professor Fred Glahe and the Institute for the opportunities and their gracious reception of my studies.

"Manichaeanism, Law, and Economics" was first published in Chalcedon's *Journal of Christian Economics*, vol. II, no. 1, Summer, 1975.

I am grateful to Mrs. Elizabeth McEachern Miller for her permission to reprint her address to the Money and Inflation Conference.

# Part One

# Chapter One

# The Meaning of Inflation

One of the great farces of our day is the supposed "war on inflation" being waged by civil governments everywhere. In every continent, politicians pledge themselves to an all-out war on inflation, conveniently neglecting to state that the immediate cause of all inflation in the modern era is the increase of the supply of money and credit by the central civil or statist agencies. Inflation is an act of state, a very highly desirable act of state from the standpoint of politicians and the bureaucracy, because it increases vastly the powers of the state. The rise of the modern totalitarian state has its economic origin in the abandonment of gold coinage for paper money. As the creator of fiat money, of instant money by means of legalized counterfeiting of wealth, the state is always the wealthiest and most powerful force in society. As inflation increases, so too does the power of the state. Every civil government thus has a vested interest in inflation. For a state to halt inflation is to diminish its power. The cry, "Stop inflation," is another way of saying, "Castrate the State," and no state or bureaucracy has yet favored its own castration.

Inflation is thus a way of life to the modern, humanistic power state, because power is its goal. The fundamental premise of modern political science is that the state is "god walking on earth." This same Hegelian (and in origin pagan) doctrine is basic to Marxism, fascism, Naziism, democracy, Fabianism, and other modern political theories. It means that the state claims *sovereignty*, an attribute of God alone, and therefore claims *the power to create*. The result of this assertion of sovereignty and the power to create is fiat laws (laws with no basis in God's law and purely arbitrary assertions of the state), fiat money (money created by state decree and having behind it the value of statist coercion), and fiat everything. Above all, it means *fiat justice*; justice ceases to be grounded in God's being and righteousness, and is grounded instead in the arbitrary judgments and decisions of the state, its bureaucracy, and its agencies.

The more humanistic the power state becomes, the more it removes its law-making policies from the elective process. The goal of the humanistic state is to replace God as the ultimate power and authority over man, and hence it works, in the name of man, to separate itself from man. Most lawmaking in the United States is not an act of Congress, or of a state legislature, but of a bureaucracy which enacts vast powers unto itself through the Federal Register or in like ways. A sovereign power is always transcendental; it transcends those whom it governs. God is beyond man and nature and separate from them; hence we speak of the supernatural. Similarly, the would-be sovereign state seeks to be transcendental, beyond man in the name of man, and its rule becomes more and more a fiat and arbitrary rule.

The goal is total power; the key or the means is money, the creation of fiat money; in brief, inflation.

When the state enters into the marketplace by means of wage and price controls, subsidies to either capital or labor or both, controls over agriculture, the creation of money and the manipulation of the money supply, or like measures, the effect on the free market is immediate. While briefly stimulating the market, it in reality depresses it, because it restricts freedom, affects prices, and creates an artificial stimulus. Thus, the real effect of state intervention in the market place and into the money supply is a depressing effect, a *depression*. The state, however, has one cure, a panacea, for all ailments, *more intervention*. The result is inflation, and an inflation, in the twentieth century, is simply a *repressed depression*. The state seeks, by means of more intervention, to undo the effect of its original intervention, and so on.

Inflation thus has a religious root. It is a consequence of the attempt by the state to play god and to resolve all human problems, not by religious and moral answers derived from the Bible, but from humanism. The state believes that, by playing god, it can abolish the problems of man and society. Instead, it aggravates those problems.

But is inflation only the work of the state? Clearly, its immediate cause is the increase of money and credit (and borrowing as well) by the state. This is very plainly true, and every attempt by statist apologists to shift the blame is false and immoral.

But granted that the immediate mechanism of inflation is in the state's monetary policy, and, granted that behind that policy is a will to power, a will to be god, do the people have no responsibility? Are they simply the innocent victims of a statist conspiracy?

Let us look briefly at an aspect of inflation which is basic to its nature. *Inflation is larceny*. By cheapening the value of money, it robs creditors and rewards debtors. Of course, the inflating state in the process makes itself the leading debtor, by deficit spending, by bond sales, and by heavy borrowings to make possible its growing bureaucracy and power. As the leading thief, the inflating state is thus congenial to all thieves, and it rewards debtors by encouraging debt: there is a benefit in income tax payments for interest payments on debt, and no benefit for saving, being self-supporting, and thrifty. In fact, such old-fashioned, Biblical morality is penalized. Thus, inflation is legalized larceny, and it is an encouragement to all of us to take part in this legalized theft. In a very real sense, the Federal Government is in the business of encouraging thieves.

When the lights went out in New York City during the 1970s, in a power failure, large numbers of black looters began a massive assault on stores, vandalizing and robbing them of millions of dollars in goods. It was, very clearly, a black mark against the Negro people; it was lawlessness and looting on a large scale. No apology or excuse for it can be valid.

However, another consideration should make us pause before we see the Negro alone as the lawless element. The black looting was simplistic, unsophisticated theft. However, those same businesses were already in the process of being looted by the Federal Government in a more sophisticated way. On top of exorbitant taxes these businesses faced the hidden taxation or theft of inflation. Their profits in prospect turned out to be less when in hand, because inflation had eaten up about ten percent of their value, a very real form of looting. The black looting in New York is occasional and limited; the statist looting is total and continuous.

But we have still to face our basic question: what is the role of the people in creating inflation? In 1936, when Franklin Delano Roosevelt was embarking on his inflationary policies, Freeman Tilden, in *A World in Debt*, wrote about the two basic facts which mark the beginnings of any inflationary program. The *first* is the intent to falsify the economic position of a nation, to doctor the books as it were, to give a false picture. This falsification means relief for the debtor at the expense of the creditor. It means pitting the have-nots against the haves, creating a clash of interest. Of course, the doctrine of the harmony of interests is derided in favor of the conflict of interests. Whether intended or not, this falsified economic picture leads to socialism and totalitarianism, because it rests on a doctrine, the conflict of interests, which posits class war; the necessity for the workers to suppress their enemies, and the need for a dictatorship to enforce a class victory. The result is either communism, Fabianism, fascism, or welfare democracy, all sisters under the same skin. Whether in a local bank or state treasury, a falsified economic position is a prerequisite to inflationary theft.

For the *second* basic fact, let us turn to Tilden's own telling words:

> Inflation, whether of bank credit or of paper currency, cannot be effective until *the larcenous purpose is generally comprehended.* This explains why in 1933 and 1934, in the United States, the credit base was enormously extended without any considerable effect upon trade or employment. The credit simply lay inert: business did not care to employ it normally, and there was not sufficient *fear* to induce its abnormal use. In this period, 1933-34, in the United States, prices rose, but not because of inflation. A similar case is observed in all paper-money expansions. At first the money makes only a short turn and goes back into the banks. Prices do not immediately rise, because the fraudulent purpose is not understood.[1]

Here we come to the heart of the matter. Inflation is larceny, and it is indeed a kind of conspiracy; it cannot work until the larcenous state (and every inflationary state is a larcenous state) has a large number of allies among the people. These allies can be rich or poor, and they do include many corporations, indeed, virtually all, and many of the poor, again virtually all. They also include many or virtually all of the middle classes, because larceny in the heart is no respecter of persons.

The inducement is this: join us in debt, says the larcenous state. Of course, as the creator of monetized debt, i.e., as an agency which can legally turn its debts into money, the Federal Government is the real gainer in all such larceny. All the same, people of all classes and corporations of all sizes find larceny appealing and profitable, and hence they encourage the state in its course and, even more, demand a larcenous course.

The larceny is, of course, disguised as charity, a concern for the social welfare, a humane public policy; a Square Deal, a New Deal, a New Frontier, and so on and on. Larceny is bad

---

[1] Freeman Tilden, *A World in Debt* (New York, NY: Funk & Wagnalls Company, 1936), 279.

enough, but theft in the name of righteousness is the ultimate in hypocrisy and self-deception.

Of course, inflation is bought in the name of goodness and social concern by the people so that they might be thieves with a good conscience. Practically, the hope is to get something for nothing, and to go into debt now in order to pay off good debts with cheap and progressively worthless money.

Meanwhile, the larcenous state and people pride themselves on having a high morality and a tender conscience. Here Tilden has a telling statement: "There is no sensibility so delicate and easily wounded as that of a person or a nation that knows it is in the wrong."[2]

A larcenous state prefers larcenous people. The income tax form clearly favors debtors rather than creditors. Should it surprise us then that the larcenous state is tender in its regard for the "rights" of a criminal, but not for the law-abiding citizen? People are of a piece morally, and the same is true of nations. No more than we can expect the Mafia to set up rescue missions for "fallen women" can we expect the larcenous state to favor the godly, productive, and law-abiding man.

This should not surprise us. Long ago, St. Augustine warned us that states without God, or without His justice, are like bands of robbers. "Justice being taken away, then, what are kingdoms but great robberies? For what are robberies (or, bands of robbers) themselves, but little kingdoms?" Augustine continued:

> The band itself is made up of men; it is ruled by the authority of a prince, it is knit together by the pact of confederacy; the booty is divided by the law agreed on. If, by the admittance of abandoned men, this evil increases to such a degree that it holds the places, fixes abodes, takes possession of cities, and subdues peoples, it assumes the more plainly the name of a kingdom because the reality is now manifestly conferred upon it, not by the removal of covetousness, but by the addition of impunity. Indeed, that was an apt and true reply which that king had asked the

---

2. *Ibid.*, 250.

man what he meant by keeping hostile possession of the sea, he answered with bold pride, "What thou meanest by seizing the whole earth; but because I do it with a petty ship, I am called a robber, whilst thou who dost it with a great fleet are styled emperor."[3]

We are best prepared to deal with a thief if we recognize him as a thief. All too many people, however, believe that the best way to deal with a larcenous state is to become thieves also, that is, debtors in an inflationary economy. They moralize it very readily. After all, they will say, my assets are being liquidated by taxation and inflation; the only way I can protect myself is to expand my holdings by debt. I will thereby nullify the effect of inflation upon me. This is trying to nullify theft by theft.

But there is a subtle evil in trying to profit by inflation. It gives a person a vested interest in the inflationary or larcenous state. Today, there are numerous wealthy and not-so wealthy conservatives who eagerly attend one conference after another on money and inflation. These conferences are very carefully advertised. Basic to their advertised appeal is the summons to "protect yourself" against inflation. The purpose of attending is to *profit* by inflation, a very different thing. One economist, who tried to teach basic *principles* of economics to such conferees found them rude and hostile. He had sought to call attention to the total immorality of inflation, when the conferees, immoral conservatives, wanted to know how to profit from it. Their excuse was self-righteous to the extreme: "I'm trying to protect myself." But protection from inflation is not a complicated matter: it involves converting one's monetary assets into gold, silver, land, a home, the tools of one's trade, and the like. These people were interested in more: like the Federal Government, they wanted to exploit inflation for their own power and profit goals. Such people soon develop a vested interest in inflation which manifests itself in their voting, and their financial support of certain candidates. For them, "conservative" and "responsible" candidates are

---

3. St. Augustine, *The City of God*, Book IV, 4. Marcus Dods translation. (New York, NY: The Modern Library, 1950), 112f.

those who use inflation to subsidize their class or group. They have become a part of the larcenous state.

Such people are no threat to the larcenous state; they are subservient allies, happy hangers-on who are ready to cash in on the larceny while sanctimoniously deploring it. They are people who want the best of both worlds, who want to eat their cake and have it too.

Such people would do well to remember, and study, the life of Cosimo di Medici, one of the great experts in the philosophy of debt as a means to power. Cosimo di Medici was a merchant and a moneylender. He owned more than two and a half tons of fine gold. He ended the wars of three states by withdrawing credit. The pope's miter was in his possession, the pope having pawned it for funds. In 1439, Cosimo di Medici became ruler of Florence. It was easy for him to rule; he appealed to the rich as their champion against equalization, and to the poor and the radicals as their hope against the rich. By encouraging debt, Cosimo di Medici gained power, because, as Solomon observed long ago, "the borrower is servant (literally, slave) to the lender" (Prov. 22:7). Cosimo di Medici enslaved a republic and a people by means of debt. Debt was to him an easy means to power, so much so that "He would have liked best, said Cosimo, to have God also among his debtors."[4] To have God in his debt would have meant to have God in his power, conforming to his policies, and playing his game! The larcenous state is an heir to Cosimo di Medici. It has nothing to fear from most of the conferees who seek "self protection." They are a part of the state's entourage.

The use of debt to enslave was not new in Solomon's day. It went back at least to the Old Babylon of Hammurabi, one of the earlier humanistic states. Basic to conquest was the role of the *tamkaru* (singular *tamkarum*), who were money-lenders, government agents, merchants, and bankers all rolled into one

---

[4.] Valeriu Marcu, *Accent on Power: The Life and Times of Machiavelli* (New York, NY: Farrar & Rinehart, 1939), 9.

package.[5] These *tamkaru* were people who encouraged debt; long before any army marched into an area, these *tamkaru* had reduced its people to economic slavery by debt. Their spirit of independence had been sapped, their character corrupted, and their economics geared to consumption rather than production. Assyria later used the same policy, and the prophet Nahum cited it as a special sin of Assyria that it had "multiplied merchants above the stars of heaven" (Nahum 3:16), i.e., had used money-lenders to promote economic slavery in one area after another. Solomon was thus commenting on an ancient and continuing practice of imperialism when he observed that "the borrower is servant to the lender" (Prov. 22:7).

The Federal Government encourages debt in a number of ways which touch the lives of every man. One is to give a tax advantage to debtors. This makes it "worth while" to go into debt. After all, there is no tax deduction for rent payments. On the other hand, if one buys a home on a 20 or 30 year note, most of the payment is in interest, and deductible, and the property tax on the house is also deductible. Very often the difference between rent and payments for comparable housing is negligible in many areas. This is certainly an inducement to go into long-term debt for housing.

Another means whereby debt is encouraged is by the expansion of the money supply by increasing the availability of credit, i.e., of borrowing. It is paradoxical that the word *credit*, coming from *credo*, I believe, has come to mean the availability of debt. A man who is a credit to his community is a man whose life is an asset to society, but to have credit increasingly means a cheaply available ability to contract debt.

Debt and inflation are closely related and interwoven. Inflation means a cheapening of money. This has been done in a variety of ways throughout history. Clipping coins, i.e., diminishing their size in order to have more gold for more

---

5. H.W.F. Saggs, *The Greatness That Was Babylon* (New York, NY: Hawthorn, 1962), 287ff.

spending, is an ancient method. Another is debasing the coinage, using baser metals exclusively, or lowering the gold or silver content. Some coinage was merely "washed" in gold or silver to give a deceptive appearance. Henry VIII's coinage was so made, and, the first point to wear on his coins being the nose on his image thereon, he became known as Old Coppernose. Another means of cheapening money is the printing of unbacked paper currency in increasing quantities, a feature of many modern inflations. More recently, another method has been brought to the forefront, increasing the availability of credit, so that people are able to buy beyond their means and in terms of an inflated period of years of debt.

This latter means of increasing the money supply points most obviously to the relationship of debt and inflation. Debt both cheapens money, and it cheapens time. Jacob agreed to work seven years for Laban, in order to accumulate a dowry to marry Laban's daughter, Rachel (Gen. 29:18). Normally, a dowry in Israel was equal to three years' income. There was thus a time factor in marriage: the necessary capital had to be accumulated first. Marriage was thus a serious and costly step, not lightly or casually taken. In modern marriage, no such time factor exists. The personal and economic, as well as social, significance of marriage has been cheapened. A young couple can move into a better home, with better furnishings, than their parents, and do it by debt. Divorce and bankruptcy provide also an easy release. Debt cheapens time. For a young man to commit himself to three or seven years of labor before marriage requires both an appreciable evaluation of the prospective bride and of his time. For a young man, however, to sign a mortgage for a house at $80,000 when an escape clause from both debt and marriage are easily available, and when inflation can in five years double the paper value of his house, is an entirely different matter. Time, debt, and the girl are all cheapened.

An old proverb, with many sources in the ancient world, declared, Let us eat, drink, and be merry, for tomorrow we die. In the twentieth century, Lord Keynes, when asked about the future, given his economics, answered in a like vein: "In the long run, we are all dead." Röpke, in commenting on the attention Keynes received for this "banal and cynical observation," wrote:

> And yet it should have been obvious that the remark is of the same decidedly unbourgeois spirit as the motto of the *ancien regime: Apres nous le deluge.* It reveals an utterly unbourgeois unconcern for the future, which has become the mark of a certain style of modern economic policy and inveigles us into regarding it as a virtue to contract debts and as foolishness to save.[6]

As Röpke pointed out, the erosion of money, and the erosion of property, go together; each promotes the other.[7] Both are linked to an erosion of the value of time. Debt and the future are nothing; the slavery of debt is nothing, "for tomorrow we die," or we walk away by declaring bankruptcy, as individuals or as a nation.

The implications of the Biblical law forbidding long-term debt begin now to emerge. It is, in part, a legislation against inflation. Several laws in the Bible deal with debt. One of these is Deuteronomy 15:1-6. Its premises and requirements, with respect to economics, include, *first*, a distinction between free men and natural slaves. The covenant man, God's man, is and must be a free man. "Where the Spirit of the Lord is, there is liberty" (2 Cor. 3:17). The covenant man must not place himself in a position of slavery or bondage: "Ye are bought with a price: be not ye the servants (or, slaves) of men" (1 Cor. 7:23). The ungodly are, however, slaves by nature; they will in some form or another enslave themselves to something, no matter how great their position may be.

*Second*, God's covenant man cannot mortgage his future: he belongs to God. As a general policy, he must, as Paul sums it up, "Owe no man anything, but to love one another" (Rom. 13:8). In the event that he must, for necessity, contract a debt,

---

[6.] Wilhelm Röpke, *A Humane Economy* (Chicago, Illinois: Henry Regnery, 1960), 100.
[7.] *Ibid.*, 19f., 191f.

it must be for a period of no more than six years. Since a
seventh year cancellation of debts between covenant men was
required, debts could not be contracted unless such a short-
term payment were clearly feasible. The future of the covenant
man, as does his whole life, belongs to God: he cannot sell
himself to men by means of debt.

*Third*, long term debts are legal for the ungodly and are not
subject to cancellation in the seventh or Sabbath year, because
all such men are by nature slaves and cannot be legislated out
of their slavery. The limitation of the term of debt is thus not
a penalty on the godly but a privilege. Freedom is their life,
their duty, and their privilege. All too many Christians view
this law (and all of the law) as a *restraint* on their freedom. For
the ungodly, it is very obviously a restraint. The entelechy of
their being is plainly described in Proverbs 8:36, where
Wisdom declares: "But he that sinneth against me wrongeth
his own soul: all they that hate me love death." The "freedom"
sought by the unbelieving is a suicidal freedom. The freedom
from debt required of the covenant man is a freedom for life,
not for death, and to view this as a restraint is insanity.

*Fourth*, freedom from debt is declared to be basic to the
elimination of poverty: "There shall be no poor among you"
(Deut. 15:4, Berkeley Version). A society which lives in terms
of God's laws concerning debt will be an inflation free society,
because it will eliminate national, institutional, family, and
personal debts. The fuel which fires inflation is the desire to
contract debts, and, at the same time, to at least partially avoid
repayment on debts. It is the desire to convert debt, a liability,
into an asset. It is, of course, as aspect of the economic
falsification that inflation produces, that debts become assets.
The state carries this to the ultimate degree: it monetizes debt.
Currency is created out of debt.[8] We have here an aspect of

---

8. See Charles Holt Carroll, *Organization of Debt into Currency, and Other
Papers* (Princeton, New Jersey: Van Nostrand, 1960). See also R.J. Rushdoony, *The Politics of Guilt and Pity* (Fairfax, Virginia: Thoburn Press,
(1970), 1978).

man's ancient dream, to be as God, and, like God, to create out of nothing (cf. Gen. 3:5).

Poverty, a form of slavery, is inescapable in an inflationary society. Inflation is a form of expropriation. The assets of creditors are expropriated by debtors. As a result, to participate in this expropriation, corporations, institutions, workers, farmers, all groups and classes enter happily into the legalized larceny. Their anticipation is that all will profit. The larcenous state, however, as the promoter of mass larceny, begins then to rob its lesser partners, with the end result that all are impoverished, and the state itself collapses. Inflation always leads to socialism or collapse. Socialism is, like inflation, a parasitic economy. When a parasite destroys a host body, the parasite also dies. Mistletoe, a parasite, can kill a tree finally, and, when it does, the mistletoe also dies. Inflation impoverishes and finally destroys all.

*Fifth*, whereas the larcenous state sees inflation and debt as the means to power, God's law states that a debt-free people and nation shall attain to true world power: "For the LORD thy God blesseth thee, as he promised thee: and thou shalt lend unto many nations, but thou shalt not borrow; and thou shalt reign over many nations, but they shall not reign over thee" (Deut. 15:6).

*Sixth*, this law of debt is a Sabbath law. The Sabbath means rest, forgiveness, a debt-free life, and the privileges of freedom.[9] The Biblical law of debt is an aspect of its anti-inflation legislation.

Another important Biblical law is Leviticus 19:35-37, which deals with just weights and measures. *Weights* in the Bible includes and often means money, since money in the Bible meant weights of gold and silver (cf. 1 Chron. 21:25). Instead of money being monetized debt, it was real wealth, in gold and silver. God indicts Judea in Isaiah 1:22 for its debased weights

---

[9.] See R.J. Rushdoony, *Institutes of Biblical Law* (Phillipsburg, New Jersey; The Craig Press, (1973) 1979).

of silver, for fraudulent money.[10] A false weight is declared by
Ezekiel to be despoiling the people, and contrary to law and
justice (Ezekiel 45:9-10).[11] Thus, any monetary standard which
departs from a 'hard' money position is injustice, and a factor
of central significance in inflation and larceny.

Of course, taxation like inflation is a means of expropriation
used by the larcenous state to confiscate wealth. Biblical law
denies to the state any taxing power other than a very limited
head or poll tax, on all males over twenty years of age, and the
same amount for all (Ex. 30:11-16). The basic social financing
is to be, not by the state but by the tithe, which must finance
religion, education, health, welfare, etc.

But, to return to the causes of inflation in the mind and heart
of man, a key factor is covetousness, something plainly
forbidden by the Tenth Commandment. To *covet* in the Bible
means to desire and to seek to gain by fraudulent means that
which belongs to another. Such a lawless possession can be
made legal by acts of state, so that covetousness can be legal
before the state. It remains always, however, an act of
lawlessness before God. St. Paul in Colossians 3:5 speaks of
covetousness as a form of idolatry. It is the idolatry of the self,
man making himself god. The covetous man does not as a
friend admire with the respect the goods of another man, or his
wife; rather, whatever he sees and wants, he seeks to possess, in
contempt of God's law. Covetousness fuels the forces which
lead to inflation. More than a little advertising appeals to
covetousness: people are encouraged to think, I deserve the
best, and then to incur debt to gain it.

Thus, "the war on inflation" is a farce. The Federal
Government creates inflation, needs it to maintain and
increase its powers, and would be castrated without it. The
people similarly like inflation: it gratifies their covetousness

---

[10.] See Gary North, *An Introduction to Christian Economics* (Phillipsburg,
New Jersey; The Craig Press (1973) 1979).
[11.] See R.J. Rushdoony, "Hard Money and Society in the Bible," in Hans
F. Sennholz, editor, *Gold is Money* (Westport, Connecticut: Greenwood
Press, 1975), 157-175.

and gives them the happy facility of committing larceny legally.

Of course, after a certain point, inflation has very unhappy consequences for all concerned, and bitterness, resentments, and hostilities increase. Then begins the morally convenient game of conspiracy hunting. The state blames the people, the "speculators," the hoarders, the easy-living mentality, the capitalists for raising prices (to meet inflation), and the workers for demanding higher wages (to cope with inflation). The people blame the state establishment, the oil companies, the bankers, and so on. Each side infers that a conspiracy exists on the other side. None will admit that their way of life requires inflation. All want the other side to "tighten its belt" and economize.

Before inflation begins, however, there must be an inflated lifestyle, or, at the least, inflated expectations about life. The inflationary mentality is geared to consumption, not production. For the inflationary mentality, being alive means having title to maximum rights, privileges, assets, and freedom, with little or no responsibility. The inflationary mentality despises God's law in favor of human rights.[12] In brief, it wants a problem-free world, which is another way of saying that the inflationary mentality chooses death, and loves it (Prov. 8:36).

---

[12.] See T. Robert Ingram, *What's Wrong With Human Rights* (Houston, Texas: St. Thomas Press, 1979).

# Chapter Two

# Regulations

Regulations are a necessary part of life. The unregulated life does not exist. The only escape from regulations is in the grave. Regulations govern us from the day of our birth. We are governed by our physical being, by the laws of God and of man, by our parents, our church, our school, our society, our friends, our callings, and by much, much more.

It is necessary to stress this fact strongly, and to keep it constantly in mind, because it is a myth, propagated by all statists, that apart from the state, man's life remains unregulated and hence lawless. Two important and equally dangerous myths are maintained by all statists as articles of faith. *First*, it is held that all life outside the state and its controlling government is unregulated life. In promoting this myth, the statists also promote a "remedy" implicit in that assertion. If all life outside the state is unregulated life, then the "answer" to that unregulated life is state regulation. To be outside the state is presupposed to be in anarchy and chaos, and to be within the state is assumed to be orderly and just. This was an article of faith in ancient paganism, so that a stateless man was seen as virtually a dead man, a man without being. Jacobsen cites an ancient Mesopotamian principle, basic to the culture of the time: "The command of the palace, like the command of Anu, cannot be altered. The king's word is right: his utterance, like that of a god, cannot be changed."[1] Given such a premise, man outside the state is in an evil condition.

This, of course, leads to the *second* myth, that the non-state-regulated life is a lawless life. Law is thus assumed to be exclusively an act of state. In terms of Biblical faith, law is the prerogative of God, not of man, because lawmaking is an attribute of sovereignty, and God alone is sovereign. However, not all regulations are laws. A law expresses, in the Biblical sense, God's justice, His demand of righteousness or justice for all men. A treaty and a contract bind only a few parties, sometimes only two. A contract between Jones and Smith has a binding force for Jones and Smith, but none for me. A contract is under law, but distinct from it. The marriage contract between my wife and myself is under law and at points potentially subject to the jurisdiction of God and the state, but my wife and I have kept that contract in faithfulness to God and without any need whatsoever for recourse to state law. My relationship to my surviving parent, my mother, is outside the state's law (but not outside God's law), but it is as regulated and lawful as possible. The non-state-regulated life is by no means a lawless life.

These two myths rest on still another myth. According to this *third* myth, the state is the agency and source of both law and morality. All law is simply enacted morality, and the state, by claiming to be the source of law, and by seeking a monopoly of law-making, declares itself to be the ground of morality and hence of law. This is, of course, a particularly dangerous assertion and myth, and is basic to the state's tacit claim to be "god walking on earth." The man or institution which is then unregulated by the state is by definition immoral. Moral status, then, becomes life under statist regulations. The result is a radical restructuring of society in

---

[1.] Thorkild Jacobsen, "Mesopotamia," in Henri Frankfort, etc., *Before Philosophy, The Intellectual Adventure of Ancient Man* (Penguin Books, (1946) 1951), 218.

terms of the moral and religious ultimacy of the state. The state, to fulfill its mission, embarks on an imperialistic crusade against men and institutions, corporations, schools, properties, and all things else, determined to save the world by statist regulations. Those who resist statist controls are seen, then, as somehow immoral and devious, as enemies and exploiters of mankind, or, at the very least, as unrealistic fools who fail to understand that morality requires state controls.

These three myths lead, *fourth*, to a significant fact: statist legislation and controls lessen the regulation of a society instead of enhancing it. Contracts, once basic to society and to commerce, were once regarded as one of the central forms of social regulation, and they were all a part of what is curiously called the private sector, i.e., of non-statist society, of the public world. Statist controls have steadily diminished the role of contracts in every area of life.

At this point, it is necessary to introduce a very real distinction which we have previously disregarded, in order to lay a broader foundation in terms of common usage. There is a very real difference between *regulations* and *controls*. *Regulation* comes from a Latin word meaning *rule*, i.e., a standard, norm, or law. *Regula*, ruler or rule, carries into the word *regulation* the concept of a norm, yardstick, or law apart from man and the state. *Control*, on the other hand, comes from a French word meaning a register, roll, or catalogue. An agency imposes controls; by its origin, regulation implies a rule of principle which governs men because they at the very least believe in it. Thus, as we examine the current scene, we must say that the modern state is unregulated by principles of supra-state validity, and is hostile to regulations and favors rather controls, more specifically, its controls. Parenthetically, we can note that the Church has also too often favored controls, church-imposed controls, instead of seeking to bring men under the regulation of God and His law by His Holy Spirit.

Thus, we must say emphatically that statist controls not only lessen the regulation of society, but work towards the destruction of regulation. Again and again in history statist controls have gone hand-in-hand with the demoralization of society and the erosion of religion.

*Fifth*, another significant fact is that statist controls not only lessen the regulation of a society, but they also lessen its freedom. The greater the element of regulation in a society, i.e., dependence on the rule of faith and principles, the greater the freedom of that society: "where the Spirit of the Lord is, there is liberty" (2 Cor. 3:17). The more we are truly governed by God's law and the Spirit of God, the less we are then governed by the state, and the greater our freedom. For the state, freedom is immoral: it means an uncontrolled life, a life outside the state and its laws. The free man becomes the immoral man, the enemy, to the statist.

The statist panacea is of course controls by the state. In 1978, apart from all municipal, county, state, and federal laws, the Federal bureaucracy added 15,452 pages to the *Federal Register*. These are all new rules designed to control every conceivable area of life. In the 1980s, the rules will increase even more. Weidenbaum notes, these controls lead to amazing requirements on companies and institutions for compliance. Thus, "One drug company's application to the FDA for approval of a skeletal muscle relaxant consisted of 456 volumes; they weighed more than a ton and stood taller than an eight-story building."[2] Such incidents are routine.

It should be apparent by now that we are strongly opposed to the vast edifice of statist controls, but believe rather in regulation by the law of God. Most people, of course, including most churchmen today, are hostile to Biblical law. Many feel apoplectic on reading of God's condemnation of their own pet sins. The Bible does have some death penalties which are very upsetting to modern man, and it leaves some men in a state of shock to learn that anyone believes in them.

The fact is, however, that a careful cataloguing of Biblical law makes clear that, *first*, God claims total jurisdiction over

---

[2.] Murray L. Weidenbaum, "Time to Control Runaway Regulation," in *Reader's Digest*, vol. 114, no. 686, June, 1979, 99.

every area of life and thought. Because He is totally God, absolutely sovereign, His law is a total law. His right to declare law is grounded on the fact that He is the Creator and the absolute Lord or property owner of all creation. We are repeatedly told that "the earth is the LORD's, and the fulness thereof; the world, and they that dwell therein" (Ps. 24:1; Ex. 9:29; Deut. 10:14; 1 Cor. 10:26).

*Second*, if we read God's law and catalogue the total number of offenses and penalties, we find that the law is readily learned, because it is a limited number of statutes, and that in many cases no man or state-imposed penalties follow upon violation of God's law. God Himself imposes the penalty in many cases, in time or in eternity, so that He limits the power of man dramatically. The powers of man and of the state can never thus be legitimately confused with the powers of God. Some very important laws thus have no prescription for any enforcement by man.

*Third*, this means plainly that the Biblical emphasis in very strongly on regulation, not on statist control. Albert Jay Nock, in *Our Enemy, the State*, spoke of ancient Israel as a government rather than a state. To a great measure, this was true. Civil government was by means of elders, heads of households, with one elder over every ten families, then elders over fifties, hundreds, thousands, etc., up to the council of seventy elders, later known as the Sanhedrin. In early Christian Europe, the College of Cardinals was, after the same pattern, made up of seventy laymen. Because the foundation of elder government was the family unit, which was also the basic regulating unit in society, the state was at most minimal.

A faith in controls is faith indeed, but it is not Biblical.

# Chapter Three

# Rationing

The Garden of Eden is often referred to as *paradise*, but the Bible never speaks of it as such. Obviously too, Adam and Eve did not consider Eden to be a paradise, because they were eventually in rebellion against it. Modern man would be even less enthusiastic about Eden.

Let us consider a few facts concerning the Garden of Eden. It was indeed an enclosed area, containing all manner of fruits, vegetables, animals, birds, and the like. But it posed certain obvious problems. *First* of all, Adam faced Eden with no tools nor capital other than his own mind and body. Moreover, Adam was ordered "to dress" and "keep" the Garden, no small task. Work obviously existed before the Fall! Adam had to develop tools, means of harvesting, and means of storage. Anyone who has worked on a farm, or tried gardening, even with the best of modern tools, will recognize Adam's problem. Granted that natural conditions before the Fall were remarkable and very different from our world today, the text of Genesis 2 still makes very clear that Adam had a very considerable task on his hands. It is very doubtful that men today would trade places with Adam, even for the prospect of the possibility of escaping death. Endless life with endless work is not the dream of modern Man! It is very plainly, however, God's promise concerning the new creation (Rev. 22:3). Hell alone is portrayed as a place with no work.

*Second*, as if this were not enough, Adam had another task, to *name* the animals (Gen. 2:19). Now in the Bible to name means to classify and define. Thus Adam was given another very considerable task, a scientific task. Since Adam began his work on Day One of human history, perhaps Day Six of creation, or soon thereafter, he had no reference library to go to, no hardware shop, and no human authorities to consult. He thus faced the most immense task in all history with no capital other than himself, and no tool, other than himself.

*Third*, with so great a task on his hands, naturally Adam felt lonely (Gen. 2:20). Yes, it was possible to feel lonely in the Garden of Eden! Thus, "paradise" had at least both very heavy work as well as loneliness, so that we are again faced with the fact that modern man would not find Eden his cup of tea. But God had a remedy for Adam's loneliness, and her name was Eve. Adam now had someone to talk to, but also someone to talk to him. Eve was created to be his helpmeet, which meant also that he now had an additional responsibility. It was his duty to feed Eve, to guide her activities, and to plan their common life. Housing was obviously necessary, because, while it did not yet rain in those days, a very heavy, rain-like mist "watered the whole face of the ground" (Gen. 2:5-6). Sleeping on the ground under such circumstances would be difficult. Probably, as soon as he was created, Adam was forced, by natural conditions, to develop some kind of housing. Since Genesis 4 tells us how, from the earliest days, farming, animal husbandry, construction, and blacksmithing, among other things, were developed to a considerable degree, very plainly Adam had quickly been forced to develop various arts and sciences.

Thus, there is nothing in the Genesis account to give us the idea that Adam lay on the ground, waiting for the fruit to fall into his mouth. There was as yet no curse upon the earth (Gen. 3:17-19), but there was work, hard work which required the application of intelligence and labor to the problems and tasks at hand. Eden had no sin, but it had problems, and they required work for their solution, intelligent work.

When that still active salesman, the tempter, stopped by to promise a no-work world, naturally Eve was interested, and so too was Adam. Capitalization and progress in God's world required work and thinking, very hard work and heavy thinking. There is a simpler way, said the salesman. Reach out to the forbidden tree: be your own god, determining for yourself what is good and evil (Gen. 3:5). The power of a god means fiat power: God speaks, and it is done; He creates out of nothing by fiat legislation. Revolt, said the salesman, and, as your own gods, embark on a course of fiat legislation and remake reality to suit yourselves.

They bought the argument, and here we are today. Men talk about freedom as though they love it, but, like Adam and Eve, they are in revolt against it. Freedom in God's world means mental and physical work and responsibility. Freedom is thus a moral fact, and who in this fallen world likes morality? Polls have shown, again and again, that most people favor wage and price controls, rationing, and fiat statist rule. Why not? The principle of man's fall is his belief that he can be his own god, and, as a god, by his fiat word create a new reality.

All of this leads to rationing. Properly understood, rationing is an inescapable fact. The word *ration* comes from a Latin word meaning *to reckon*, or *calculate*. Air cannot be rationed; God has so created it that it is available to all men. Men can pollute it, or purify it, but they cannot ration it (although, given the statist mentality, someone is bound to try it someday!). Automobiles and houses, however, are rationed, as are food, clothing, books, and most things in our lives.

Rationing is by two means. *First*, rationing is by pricing. The price of goods is the oldest and only successful means of rationing in the world. Perhaps the greater majority of mankind would like a large, well-furnished, and attractive house, but most do not have the price required to have one. In a free society, prices do the rationing. Men then work and save in terms of certain objectives. My wife and I long dreamed of a good home in the country; we went for years without many things, have always bought used cars, and we now have a place in the mountains. Others we know chose other things, including many things appealing to us, but not in our minds as important as our house and land. We have what we worked and planned for, what labor and intelligence led us to gain. By the price factor, we were rationed; certain things, however desired, were off the market for us. We were limited in the variety of things we could buy, and, in buying what we chose, limited as to how good a home, or how much land, we could acquire.

Prices thus are the only effective means of rationing. Price determines at every point the quality of the item, the availability, and the quantity, among other things.

Price represents both work and intelligence. Every item which enters the market represents work, but it also represents intelligence. Work and intelligence, however, do not guarantee sales. There are still a few excellent buggy-makers in the United States; one is only eleven miles from us, across the canyon, but the market for buggies in limited. The market sets the price and rations the goods. Thus, we have no glut of buggies. If a buggy-maker overproduces buggies, he is soon bankrupt and out of business.

The *second* means of rationing is by state controls. The state, or the people of the state, believe that everyone should have good housing, and plenty of milk, eggs, and meat. Controls are introduced to place these and other items within the reach of all men. Why should any man, even remotely, face Adam's hardships? Of course, few, rather, none, today face as difficult a situation as did Adam. Modern man's situation is not as difficult, but it is, unlike Adam's, complicated by the fact of man's sin. Man wants the fiat world promised by that old salesman, and still promised by his present-day salesmen in church, state, and press. Why, in the world of "plenty" should any man lack anything?

Adam, of course, lacked everything, even in the Garden of Eden. He was not created to be a god, but to be a man, a creature, and his only means of capitalization was work and intelligence. The rationing Adam faced was a severe one, because he inherited nothing from the past, whereas we are born into a world of houses, stores, tools, and accumulated knowledge, a tremendous and too seldom appreciated capitalization.

When the state seeks to ration goods, it controls the market; it affects or controls prices, and also wages. The result is shortages. Eggs or milk for all sounds fine, but, until the state, like Christ, can multiply loaves and fishes, i.e., create out of nothing, it destroys price and therefore production by its intervention. Who can afford to produce at a loss? But controls do lead to the destruction of rationing by price. As a result, in the name of providing for all, all are denied the availability of the goods.

The issue in rationing is more than a moral issue: it is theological. The question is: Who is God? The state has its answer to that question. The Christian cannot in good conscience agree. Capitalization is not by the "divine" state's fiat decree. The nature of reality has not changed since Adam's day. Man, by his fall, has indeed changed, but the reality he must live with remains the same.

# Chapter Four

# The Economics of Satan

That old traveling salesman of quackery, Lucifer, also known as Satan, is a great purveyor of nostrums, not only religious but economic as well. We have seen how he found the economics of Eden to be repulsive. As he surveys world history, Satan finds the economic handicaps imposed upon man by God to be insufferable. As a result, he offers a "better" plan.

Now we must remember that Satan sees himself as "an angel of light" (2 Cor. 11:14). He was no doubt the original bleeding heart liberal: he decided on his own what was good for mankind, and, because he was the champion of self-created good, he was by inference himself the soul of goodness, "an angel of light." Naturally, the polite or impolite inference also was that God is a God of darkness.

This "righteous" purveyor of light and goodness was on hand at a pivotal moment of history, when Jesus Christ was in the wilderness. The Bible, and Christendom generally, speak of the event as *the temptation in the wilderness.* Satan presented it as the great opportunity, the opportunity of the ages. The first temptation was economic. More recently, some of Satan's more modest followers have offered five-year plans, or, with

U.S. presidents, who are limited by a term of office, four-year plans. Satan's plan was for all of history, and it is the foundation of all economic planning. As Matthew, a reformed and converted tax-collector (not many of those around these days) reports it:

> 3. And when the tempter came to him, he said, If thou be the Son of God, command that these stones be made bread.
> 4. But he answered and said, It is written, Man shall not live by bread alone, but by every word that proceedeth out of the mouth of God. (Matt. 4:3-4).

*First*, it should be noted that in the Greek text Satan actually said, "If thou be a (not *the*) Son of God." His inference was that Jesus was one son among many, all men and angels being supposedly sons of God. At most, Satan inferred, there is a position of equality.

*Second*, the temptation was, "command that these stones be made bread." Calling attention to the rocky wilderness, and to the world hunger, Satan demanded a solution to that hunger. The world's economic problems were more serious then than now. Satan's plain inference was that God's plan for man is heartless, and has been heartless from Day One in Eden. How can a just God expect man to have any religious feelings about Him, when He sets man in a garden and in a world where man's major time factor and occupation is the brutal question of economic survival? How can God and religion be central to man's life when providing for one's daily bread controls man's daily life? Because of God's plan, man's life, instead of being a religious pilgrimage, becomes "a rat race." The economics of Eden were demeaning to Adam, and, from Satan's perspective, man's economic prospects have not improved since then.

A God with total power, and a Savior with like power, has one obvious duty: to answer the economic problem. Turn these stones into bread, and solve man's key crisis and conflict. I have the perfect economic plan, the old quack declared: *free man from economic want*. The key to the good society is the elimination of this brutal necessity for work. The economic freedom given to man from Eden on is a ruthless and cruel one;

for the majority of mankind, it means want and exploitation. The economic problem must precede the religious problem. Before men can be saved, they must be fed.

If this sounds like modern liberation theology, it is because they are identical. Liberation theology says that a socialist economic redistribution and solution must precede religious salvation. To talk about salvation in Jesus Christ to hungry and needy peoples is evil to liberation theologians. Some liberation theologians object to the violence and revolution of Marxism, but not to its economic policies.[1] Such men refuse to acknowledge that it is the economics of Marxism, more than its wars and revolutions, which are its major and key form of war and violence. It is the economics of Marxism also which is its massive method of injustice. However, another liberationist, Ruben Alves, has an answer to this. For him "human freedom (the possibility of creativity, man as subject) rather than justice is the dominant element in his view of liberation."[2] It must be very comforting to men in Soviet slave labor camps that man himself, not justice, is freedom! Costas tells us that liberation theology starts with poverty-stricken man, not with God.[3] But if it starts with man rather than God, it is not theology but anthropology. Moreover, to make a *need* the ultimate norm and value by which all things are judged is the ultimate in moral debasement. It is also the economics of Satan: "Command that these stones be made bread" and feed the world's hungry peoples. Liberation theology goes much lower than God and heaven to find its doctrines. Clark H. Pinnock tells us, "The handwriting is on the wall. The words of the prophets are on the subway walls. Let us arise and seek God's kingdom and his justice."[4] If this seems like a new low

---

[1.] Piero Gheddo, *Why is the Third World Poor?* (Maryknoll, NY: Orbis Books, 1973), 16f.

[2.] Jose Miguez Bonino, *Doing Theology in a Revolutionary Situation* (Philadelphia, Pennsylvania: Fortress Books, 1975), 75.

[3.] Orlando E. Costas, *The Church and its Mission: A Shattering Critique from the Third World* (Wheaton, Illinois: Tydale House, 1974), 224.

[4.] Clark H. Pinnock, "A Call for the Liberation of North American Christians," in Carl E. Armerding, editor, *Evangelicals and Liberation* (Phillipsburg, New Jersey, Presbyterian and Reformed Publishing Company, 1977), 136.

in theological sources and wisdom, just wait. Report has it that the new word will come from toilet walls.

How far churchmen are ready to go is apparent in the thinking of the Jesuit scholar, Christopher F. Mooney, formerly president of Woodstock College and then Visiting Scholar at the Yale Law School. Mooney comments in *Man Without Tears*, on Dostoyevsky's tale of Satan, appearing in time as the Grand Inquisitor, in *The Brothers Karamazov*:

> Christ returns to the scene of the Spanish Inquisition and is accused of offering to man gifts he is incapable of accepting. Man cannot live with riches such as freedom and love, the Inquisitor says, but can be happy only with authority and bread. Freedom and responsibility are burdens too heavy to bear.[5]

This sounds good, but Mooney has not disowned either the Inquisitor or Jesus. He notes, "The judgment of Dostoevsky's Inquisitor may have been accurate in a former age; it is much less so today, and it may be totally false tomorrow."[6] The means to this change is not regeneration but one of "abolishing one mode of being human and creating another, whether this involves structures in a given society or certain styles of human behavior."[7] In other words, man is going to be *made* free by restructuring either society, or man, or both. This is hardly the world of Jesus Christ, in which man, being regenerated by God, changes his world to conform to God's world. Rather, it is the statist humanistic vision of the restructuring of both man and society.

Of course, we are told to accept this coercive restructuring of ourselves as benevolent, because these statist agents tell us they are benevolent! Frank L. Field, of the Counseling Center, the University of California at Santa Barbara, wants compulsory camps for this restructuring. He assures us that there is "a tremendous difference" between "the typical

---

[5.] Christopher F. Mooney, *Man Without Tears* (New York, NY: Harper & Row, (1973) 1975), 30.
[6.] *Ibid.*, 34.
[7.] *Idem.*

concentration-camp" and "proposed reeducative centers."[8]
What is the "tremendous difference"? Simply that "powerful
control over individual behavior is not necessarily evil or
antidemocratic" when the right group is doing the
controlling.[9] What a noble sentiment! I do not recall that any
tyrant ever failed to call himself the source of justice, goodness,
and light. Stalin and Hitler were both self-assured of their
rightness and righteousness, as is virtually every bureaucrat in
Washington, D.C., London, Moscow, Peking, and elsewhere.
Educators like Fields have no monopoly on a self-assured truth
and righteousness.

Can we be blamed for being reminded of that Old Quack's
program, every man his own god, with his own private
doctrines of good and evil, right and wrong (Gen. 3:5)?

The temptation, "Command that these stones be made
bread," is a demand that man be allowed to remain as he is, and
to evade work, freedom, and responsibility, and to have his
environment or world transformed to please him. God and the
world make demands of men. Men want instead a universe in
which God and the environment give men signed blank checks
on which demand payment can be made at will. The
economics of Satan is an economics of demand and coercive
payment. The pay-off, however, is that finally all the payments
fall due on those who make the demands.

But, *third*, our Lord answers the Old Quack: "It is written,
man shall not live by bread alone, but by every word that
proceedeth out of the mouth of God." The root problem is not
economic: it is moral, and it is religious. Man's main problem
is not hunger, it is himself, and his sin. Hunger is indeed real,
but man is more than an economic animal; he is a religious
creature. The hunger of the ill-fed is at least matched by the
hunger and misery of the well-fed. The well-fed have a very
high suicide rate.

---

8. Frank L. Field, *Freedom and Control in Education and Society* (New
York, NY: Thomas Y. Crowell, 1970), 48.
9. *Ibid.*, 50.

Our Lord quotes from Moses in making His reply, from Deuteronomy 8:3, which reads in part that God "suffered thee (Israel) to hunger...that he might make thee to know that man doth not live by bread only, but by every word that proceedeth out of the mouth of the LORD doth man live." Both manna and hunger had as their purpose this goal and this knowledge.

When economics becomes a branch of politics, it ceases to be economics and becomes messianic. It becomes an instrument of power whereby men play god and plan to use human beings as their raw material for creating an imaginary world and imaginary man. It becomes then the economics of Satan, still a revolt against Eden and what Eden represented. The temptation of Eden is still with us, and it is still evil.

# Chapter Five

## Shortages

Like most people of my age, I had a good education, that is, I was fed all the liberal myths and illusions as gospel truth, and I was fed them ably. I was just beginning junior high school, at the beginnings of the 1930s, when I was taught that, by the time I would be twenty-one years old, the world's coal and oil deposits would be exhausted. I was warned that it was necessary for my generation to face up to the fact of this coming world disaster. Of course, the world's total known deposits of coal and oil were far less than they are now, but the same horror story of a world blackout, of a cold and energy-less world population, is still with us.

In recent years, I have spoken to this junior high indoctrination to a number of people, of my age and younger. Perhaps, I reasoned, I had a few teachers of rather dim outlook, and others may have been better taught. To the contrary, I found that such teaching has been commonplace from at least the 1930s to the present.

I hardly need add that it is very prevalent today. Such thinking has been well answered in a number of able books.[1] We live in a world of disaster by expectation, and disaster by state decree.

There is, for all such people, a scareful and alarming fact about creation: there is a built-in scarcity. Earlier, humanism tended to operate on the premise of infinite resources; in the twentieth century, especially after mid-century, opinion began to favor the scarcity doctrine.

Now it is true this world is a limited world. Infinity and infinite power and resources belong only to God. The very fact of creatureliness limits both man and the universe. Man finds this a disaster only because he dreams of being as God, and to be anything less is for him an evil.

To live in the world God made is to live in a world of shortages *which only man can relieve.* Adam faced a world of radical shortages on Day One of man's history, a shortage of tools, of housing, of furnishings, of tableware, of everything. True, he had a garden full of fruit, but no stepladder, and no bucket or bushel basket. Have you ever tried to shinny up a fruit tree with a naked butt? Anyone who has ever picked peaches knows how fuzzy peaches are on a tree, and how that fuzz clings to the flesh and itches; there is no relief short of bathing. A scratched and itchy Adam must have spent more than a little time cleaning up in one or another of Eden's four rivers, Pison, Gihon, Hiddekel, and Euphrates. No doubt, more than once, before his first meal and after, he must have wondered why God did not provide him with more equipment. The Landlord had placed him in a situation of appalling shortages.

Of course, it was intentional. The potentialities in the world are, while not infinite, more than man can ever develop in the

---

[1.] See, for example: John Maddox, *The Doomsday Syndrome*, New York, NY: McGraw-Hill, (1972) 1973; and Melvin J. Grayson and Thomas R. Shephard, Jr., *The Disaster Lobby, Prophets of Ecological Doom and other Absurdities*, Chicago, Illinois: Follet, 1973.

long history of time. To be developed, those potentialities require work and intelligence, and a progressive capitalization. The key, as Edward A. Powell points out, is finding where the potentialities are.

Disaster faced the world of the 19<sup>th</sup> century, with its radical dependency on whale oil, until oil was first discovered and brought out of the earth. Since then, a series of previously once unknown or unimagined potentialities have led to new sources of power, energy, and technology.

From Eden on, the world has always faced potential or actual shortages. Economic progress means overcoming shortages by applied intelligence and work.

One area of total shortage facing Adam in Eden was money. None existed. This was only natural, of course. Before there can be money, there must be work; there must be the production of wealth, and exchange by means of a trustworthy medium of exchange, which is gold. Not surprisingly, two verses in Genesis 2, vv. 11 and 12, tell us where gold was to be found.

Modern, fiat money represents wealth, just as a snapshot represents a house or a man pictured therein, but it is neither. This is why it always inflates and becomes progressively worthless. Sound money does not merely represent wealth; it is wealth. The gold ruble of the tsars is still valued money, but their paper money is worthless except as a curio.

Gold as money, like every other form of wealth, has a price; it costs something to mine and refine. In brief, it is costly money. However, the goal of the humanitarian statists is *costless money*. The value of the costless money to men is that it enables the state to enact legislation and controls with powers previously unobtainable except by brute force, and inadequately even then. Costless money appears as a bonanza for all, a means of eating one's cake and having it too.

J. Freire d'Andrade, in commenting on our modern, costless paper money, observed, with respect to its consequences:

First: work is not the only way to earn a living. Secondly: work can receive a value independently of the worth society attributes to the services rendered. That is, a situation arises where we have no voice, as individual members of society, in setting the value of the work of others.[2]

Costless money is state money, state capital, and it leads to state-ordained projects, and state-controlled economics. This is now not only a national but an international fact of economic life, because people are taxed directly and indirectly by inflation, to provide for world growth, and, supposedly, world economic stability. As a result, we face a world of government-made economic structures where, in d'Andrade's words, "all countries have built the life of their communities upon an entirely artificial structure."[3]

One of the purposes of costless money is to relieve world hunger and eliminate shortages. One of its consequences, finally, is to create massive and sometimes artificial shortages and hunger. The shortages are artificial when goods are withheld finally from the market, or go to the market in inferior form, because the money is becoming worthless.

Production is perverted by a number of causes, but on the whole and in the main, by statist policies and intervention. War can pervert production dramatically by creating artificial barriers and artificial markets within those barriers. Debt also perverts production, often dramatically, and certainly, since World War II, this has been a major factor in preventing production. Finally, costless money is the decisive and continuing form of perverting production.

It does more than pervert production. It perverts and destroys civil orders, rulers, and nations. It has not been sufficiently stressed that Louis XVI, in refusing to follow the counsel of Turgot, his finance minister, that there be "No bankruptcies, no new taxes, no loans" ensured his own

---

[2] J. Feire d'Andrade, *Freedom Chooses Slavery* (New York, NY: Coward-McCann, 1959), 61.
[3] *Ibid.*, 54.

downfall. In dismissing Turgot, he dismissed his own future, an act of dismissal being repeated everywhere today. It was to Napoleon's credit that he refused that course and told his first cabinet, "I will pay cash or nothing." Napoleon held "National debt as immoral and destructive, silently undermining the basis of the state; it delivers the present generation to the execration of posterity." Moreover, he held, "While I live, I will emit no paper," meaning both bonds and paper money.[4] Not surprisingly, Napoleon had no popularity with the other powers of his day.

Weber, in his excellent study, *Grow or Die!*, comments, "In essence, to say that we are running out of resources means, according to sociologist Ben J. Wattenburg, that "the one key resource – the intellect of man – is running dry. But that is not happening."[5] What we do have a shortage of is the morality to resist the economics of Satan, to resist costless money, debt, and statist nostrums. We want men and the world to be saved by shortcuts and by fiat answers devised by man.

Shortages are less a problem now than they were in Eden. The problem is man, and man is a sinner. He dreams of being god, of creating out of nothing, so that he can have something for nothing. He governs his life, his economics, and his politics in terms of that dream. Century after century, he has attempted to impose his statist dream (or nightmare) on history, only to create disaster upon disaster. He will not learn; he refuses to learn. After all, you can teach a god nothing. Only when man becomes again a man in Jesus Christ, when he surrenders the madness of his dream to be god, can he deal, by means of intelligence and work, with the problem of shortages. The problem is at root a moral problem, and it requires a moral answer.

---

[4.] Tilden, *A World in Debt*, 221, 248, 313, 323.
[5.] James K. Weber, *Grow or Die!* (New Rochelle, NY: Arlington House, 1977), 61.

# Chapter Six

## Morality and Economics

A resolution adopted by the trustees of the Institute for Monetary Research, in Washington, D.C., September 11, 1970, reads:

> RESOLVED: That the essence of the money problem is more moral than technical – that as money is the standard of economic value and measure of commerce the manipulation of money is evil, whether in the interest of creditors or debtors, industry or labor, producers or consumers, government or taxpayers; that the integrity of money should be maintained by clearly defined content and composition, and by adherence to the definition.

This position is one which the Institute's executive director, Dr. Elgin Groseclose, has maintained for many years in his excellent writings.

Economics is inseparable from morality. Bad economics is simply theft in the name of goodness. I have had occasion to speak to and with criminals, in and out of prison, and once took a man, paroled as a narcotics pusher, from one state to another. I found that thieves and criminals have an amazing talent for self-justification, but their talents are slight when compared to those of socialists. The socialist glows with self-

47

righteousness when he proposes or enacts theft; he is, after all, only taking what was "wrongfully" acquired, by his definition.

But theft is theft, even if we steal from an actual thief. Theft is not eliminated by indirection; it is still theft, if I ask another man, or the state, to do it for me. It is also still theft, even if I have a noble purpose in mind for the proceeds of the theft.

When we choose hard money or fiat money, self-regulation or controls, rationing by the state or by price, or whatever other policy decision we make, we are making moral decisions. Moreover, economics began in the Garden of Eden.

Adam had moral-economic decisions at every turn: to work hard, or to perform minimal work; to act as God's steward in the Garden, or to treat it as a personal wealth to be used at will; and so on. On man's creation, God had commanded man, saying: "Be fruitful, and multiply, and replenish the earth, and subdue it: and have dominion over the fish of the sea, and over the fowl of the air, and over every living thing that moveth upon the earth" (Gen. 1:28). *The creation or dominion mandate* to man, given in Genesis 1:26-28, is a religio-economic command. Man in Eden was given a task of religio-economic development which was to set a prototype for the whole earth. Thus, while Adam's initial activity was to be limited to Eden, the creation mandate speaks of the entire world as the goal of the mandate. This mandate is repeated to Noah after the Flood (Gen. 9:1-17), given for a limited area to Joshua for Palestine (Joshua 1:1-9), and again set forth in terms of the world by our Lord in Matthew 28:18-20.

Unhappily, few churchmen are interested in the creation mandate. Moreover, their doctrine of morality is limited to a few "thou shalt nots," some of which are church-ordained rather than God-given.

But man has a calling to subdue the earth and to exercise dominion over it. This is not a destructive calling, but a constructive one. We are to use the natural world under God, not worship it. Nature-worship has propagated all kinds of myths. One such myth is the idea of "virgin soil" as somehow good until raped by men. After Day One, no virgin soil existed. America, for example, saw much destruction before the coming of the white man. The buffalo herds of the West ate all grass down to the ground, and they created dust fields that led to dust storms visible at great distances. Other parts of the country had even worse problems: soil soured by pine needles, soil so compacted by centuries of no cultivation and animal traffic that a pick was needed to penetrate it. It is a difficult, costly, and painful task to bring "virgin soil" into production. Despite some areas of abuse, most farmland in the United States is better now than before Columbus, and has increased in productivity with each generation.

True, some forests have disappeared, but others have been remade by man. Tree production is an important form of farming in the United States, far more than most people realize. The focus, in any case, cannot be animals or trees, but rather God's requirement that the earth be made fruitful as the Kingdom of God. The focus is not on the trees or animals, nor on man. The original and best rules of conservation are in the Bible.[1]

But, to return to Adam: the economic development of the earth as God's Kingdom was to begin in the Garden of Eden. God, in giving His law through Moses, made clear how important that development is to Him: laws are given governing property, land, mortgages, sales, interest, weights, measures, economic liability, restitution, foods, and much, much more. The importance of economics in the Bible can only be eliminated by eliminating God's law, and all subsequent comments on it by prophets, apostles, and our Lord. However, when we do this, we make our religion irrelevant, and a stench in God's nostrils.

The subject of economics was once taught as "moral economy." The separation of Christian morality and economics has done neither any good. Economics has not

---

[1.] See R.J. Rushdoony, *The Institutes of Biblical Law*, vol. 1 (Phillipsburg, New Jersey: The Presbyterian and Reformed Publishing Co. [1973] 1994).

ceased to be a moral concern, but it has become a humanistic moral concern. Instead of the governing and providential hand of God, we now have the moral government of the humanistic state. In the realm of economics, the state has become the source of morality rather than the triune God. The result is the power state, or the god-state.

Man now faces an increasingly powerful state whose growth threatens and destroys man's life and freedom. Back in the 1940s, a cattleman proposed to me a simple solution to the problem of statism: Castrate the state, or else it will castrate you.

Anti-statism is a powerful force today, insofar as numbers are concerned, but an impotent factor in world politics. The reason is that the very people who look at the growth of statism with horror are also those who either 1) look to the state for moral solutions or answers, or 2) look to the state for subsidies and aid. Their hostility is the resentment of the slave mind for slavery. The slave mind hates freedom, but it merely resents slavery.

The state is not God; it is neither a creator, able by its fiats to give something more than it receives, nor the source of true morality and true law in any society. The state is our own sins writ large.

Thus, some would have us treat Internal Revenue Service men as lepers. Most I.R.S men are perhaps deservedly to be classified as moral lepers, but from whom did they contract the disease? The I.R.S is the creation of envious taxpayers, ready to see the rich robbed, but forgetting that, when we legalize and unleash theft, the poorer and middle classes are usually the easier victims. The moral disease of the I.R.S. is one contracted from society at large, and the cure must begin there.

# Chapter Seven

## Larceny in the Heart

A friend, Ted Muscio, made a trip last winter into an old and historic mining town, a county seat. A neighbor, in his nineties, asked Ted Muscio to check on his grandfather's grave while there, and to see what had happened to the old family home. When mining began in the 1890s, they left town, simply abandoning their home, which, like others, sat vacant. Ted located the house, with its Victorian "gingerbread," and checked on history in the county records. In 1942, it had been sold for back taxes and costs. The lone bidder had refused to pay a cent more than back taxes and costs and thus gained the house for $6.46. Amazing? Before inflation, in the early 1900s, many houses in the West were built for $300. For $1,000, a very superior house could be built. Yesterday, I read Alvin M. Josephy, Jr., *Black Hills, White Skies*, (1978), a pictorial "history" of the Black Hills of South Dakota, from their settlement to World War I. On p. 195 is pictured a large, four-story, turreted sandstone building, the Gillespie Hotel, at Hot Springs, called then an American Carlsbad and "a mecca for visitors from all over the country." The popular Gillespie Hotel was built by Fred Gillespie in 1890 for $25,000.

Some of the homes built in an earlier era for $300 have sold, in some larger cities and desired locations, for over $80,000 in recent years. The reason, of course, is inflation. Inflation is an increase in the money supply by the increase of credit (or debt), by bonds or borrowing, and by printing press money. The house which had been bought for $6.46 had a new roof, which may have cost more than the original price of the home, and all subsequent maintenance.

Now, behind the increase in the money supply, is, as we have seen, planned larceny by the state and the citizenry, the voters. For inflation to succeed, Freedman Tilden held, its larcenous purpose must be understood and shared by the people. But it must be stated even more clearly that inflation begins where people have larceny in their hearts.

Helmut Schoek, in *Envy* (1966), called attention to the deadly role played in society by envy. Envy demands the leveling of all things, because the envious man finds superiority in others intolerable. He sees it better to turn the world into hell rather than to allow anyone to prosper more than himself, or to be superior to him. Envy negates progress. On the other hand, as Schoek noted, "the more both private individuals and the custodians of political power in a given society are able to act as though there were no such thing as envy, the greater will be the rate of economic growth and the number of innovations in general."[1] The envious man wishes to level and equalize, and he turns envy into 'virtue' by calling it a demand for fraternity and equality. Since, however, a strictly equalitarian society is impossible, it follows, Schoek pointed out, that "the envious man is, by definition, the negation of the basis of any society."[2] Envy creates a conflict society in which the evil men are held to be precisely the most successful and advanced members of society. Their crime is their success, their wealth, or their superiority. Envy is justified by many sociologists and social scientists, and envy

---

[1]. Helmut Schoek, *Envy, A Theory of Social Behaviour* (New York, NY: Harcourt, Brace & World, 1966), 11.
[2]. *Ibid.*, 26.

becomes then a fertile and justified cause of vandalism, rioting, and crime. Hatred and resentment are justified and made marks of a "social conscience." The result is class warfare and a conflict society in which the rise of hostility and envy are seen as steps towards social progress, when in fact they lead to disaster.

Of course, envy has deep roots in history and is an aspect of man's original sin. *First* of all, the tempter, in approaching Eve, played on the difference between God and man as an evil. God, he held, is trying to prevent man from reaching a position of equality with Him. "*Got doth know* that in the day ye eat thereof, then your eyes shall be opened, and ye shall be as gods, knowing good and evil" (Gen. 3:5). Every man has a right to be his own god, he held, determining for himself what constitutes good and evil. Authoritarianism, the tempter held, must be abolished and equality instituted. Why should Adam and Eve labor like peons in the Garden, with not even housing provided, while God reigns at ease in heaven? Arise, ye prisoners of paradise! You have nothing to lose but your chains.

*Second*, the tempter shrewdly spoke to Eve, doubly under authority, God's and Adam's. Why should Adam have any authority over her? Both need liberation from God, and Eve needed liberation from Adam.

*Third*, Adam was equally fretful over responsibility. Why should he make all the decisions, in the final analysis? If his first attempt at housing was a sorry affair, why should he be responsible for providing it, while Eve played the judge and critic? People envy, not only their "superiors" for their power, but their "inferiors" for their very limited responsibility and liability. One large employer some years ago welcomed the controls over his employment practices (hiring, firing, etc.) by the union. His comment was, "Why should I have to make all the decisions and take all the blame?" It was much easier to sit back and complain about the union!

*Fourth*, when confronted by God, both Adam and Eve refused to accept responsibility. Adam blamed both Eve and God: "The *woman* whom *thou* gavest to be with me, she gave me of the tree, and I did eat" (Gen. 3:12). Similarly, Eve blamed the tempter: "The serpent beguiled me, and I did eat" (Gen. 3:13). Both pleaded innocence and accused others of a conspiracy against themselves.

The same is true of modern man's approach to inflation: the evil one is Washington, D.C., the international bankers, or anyone other than themselves. Men whose lives are geared to inflationary living, and who run from one conference to another, unconcerned about the destruction to their country by inflation but eager to learn of a new way to make money out of inflation, will with consummate hypocrisy sit back and blame the politicians or bankers for inflation. True, politicians and bankers have their guilt, but who demands inflation from them by their envy, their debt-living, and their heart full of larceny? Is it not the voters?

Inflation begins where there is larceny in the heart. The only long-term cure for it is honesty in the heart. Impossible? Our Lord said, "With men this is impossible, but with God all things are possible" (Matt. 19:26). Political cures only worsen a situation. For a changed society, changed men are necessary. If men discount this answer, we are entitled to suspect that they want the virtues of Phariseeism, the "right" to condemn the Federal Government for its inflationary policies, together with the "right" to operate freely with larceny in the heart. Of such is not the Kingdom of God.

# Chapter Eight

# Inflation and the Love of Money

According to D.B. Knox, "The view of the Old Testament and of the New Testament is that wealth is a blessing from God."[1] A statement like that is very upsetting to many modern churchmen, who are bent on establishing wealth as a mark of sin. Some ministers have maintained that to make more than $30,000 a year is sinful; other churchmen, whose salaries perhaps approach that sum, have set the sinful level somewhat higher! Abraham, blessed by God, was made rich (Gen. 13:2). Psalm 112:1-3 declares,

> 1.Praise ye the LORD. Blessed is the man that feareth the LORD, that delighteth greatly in his commandments.
> 2.His seed shall be mighty upon the earth: the generation of the upright shall be blessed.
> 3.Wealth and riches shall be in his house: and his righteousness endureth forever.

Men are called to be faithful in the use of wealth (Luke 16:11), and to be liberal towards those in need (1 Tim. 6:18). Riches are a blessing to be enjoyed, but with a sense of responsibility (1 Tim. 6:17-18). We are not to trust in our wealth but in the Lord

---

[1]. D.B. Knox, "Wealth" in J.D. Douglas, editor, *The New Bible Dictionary* (Grand Rapids, Michigan: Wm B. Eerdmans, (1962) 1973), 1319.

(Ps. 62); those who trust in their wealth or riches are denounced (Luke 6:24-25; James 5:1-6), and their trust is productive of evil.

However, the Bible does *not* say that wealth leads to sin; rather, man's sinful heart *uses* wealth at times to increase the scope of its sin.

Moreover, it becomes clear from 1 Timothy 6:9-10, that, when "riches" are condemned, it is a particular kind of wealth, or, to be precise, *the love* of a particular form of wealth, money. Paul declares,

> 9. But they that will be rich fall into temptation and a snare, and into many foolish and hurtful lusts, which drown men in destruction and perdition.
> 10. For the love of money is the root of all evil: which while some have coveted after, they have erred from the faith, and pierced themselves through with many sorrows. (1 Tim. 6:9-10)

(In the parable of Luke 12:15-21, it is not wealth but *covetousness* which is condemned. Covetousness is a sin which strikes rich and poor alike.)

Why is the *love of money*, and not other forms of wealth, condemned? Why not the love of large farms or ranches, or a prosperous business? If we miss this point, we miss a basic fact of Scripture.

The *love* of money is essentially a love of irresponsible wealth and power. If I have a million dollars in hard money, I am rich in a particular way. My use of that money *can* be responsible, but, even then, the responsibility is a rather two-edged thing. Most men who are rich in money are responsible to themselves, not to God nor to men, and more than a few are irresponsible to themselves and their future, i.e., their family.

If I have land as my wealth, that land is *only* a source of wealth if it is productive. Money loaned out can stimulate the economy and be productive to that degree, but the production is incidental, not basic. My love of a ranch or a farm, a business, or a production center, is the love of a directly producing form of wealth. I am then involved in the *responsible use of wealth*, and the *responsible production of wealth*. My wealth is then future-oriented, not present or consumption oriented.

In the world of pagan antiquity, men, lacking the limited but real restraints later imposed by the Church Fathers and Christianity had an inordinate distrust of monetary wealth and therefore of its means of self-perpetuation, interest, or usury. Their ban on usury (unsuccessfully) was wrong, but their fears of monetary wealth were well-grounded. The insane display, irresponsible conduct, and moral degeneracy which accompanied monetary wealth led pagan moralists to condemn its ability to survive by means of interest (a wrong solution), but their fears represented a clear perception of a moral fact: monetary wealth is readily irresponsible and potentially a danger in society.

The Bible, however, does *not* say that the problem is money, but the *love* of money, i.e., the love of irresponsible wealth and power.

Consider the social implications of a *love* of money. It creates, not a production-oriented, but consumption-governed society. Where men are governed, in their desire for wealth, by a love of the land, or of commerce, or industry, they will be working and productive members of society. In their industry, they will be working and productive members of society. In their health, they will seek freedom for production, for the market-place, from statist controls. In their decline, they will seek protection and subsidies, but they will still be production oriented.

When, however, men are governed by a love of money, they will be consumption and leisure oriented. They will demand a social order which produces more money, because money is at the top of their list of priorities. This means, of course, an inflationary society. All segments of society want welfarism; the indigent will take it in the form of outright hand-outs. Others will receive their welfare checks and "free" money in more respectable ways. By means of inflation and debt, they will expand their holdings and pay off good debts with bad money, a disguised form of subsidy and welfarism. Not only civil government but most corporations have become adept at this form of welfarism. The welfare cheating by the poor is amateurish by comparison.

Let us look again at Paul's statement. He does not say that the love of money is our key and original sin. That central sin is the desire to be our own god (Gen. 3:5). Rather, Paul tells us, that this sin, the love of money, is the root of all evil in society, in its implications in the lives of men. The whole point of 1 Tim. 6:9-10 is, *first*, to warn against this love of money, and, *second*, to call attention to what it does to men.

The word translated as *evil* is in the Greek *kakos*, a word which has a very ancient and continuing usage in Greek and other Indo-European languages: it means feces. Very bluntly, Paul says the *love* of money, not money itself, but the love (and hence the people possessed by such a love) of money is the source of all shit in a social order.

It warps society from production to consumption; it produces inflation; and it dirties the whole of civilization with evil, *kakos*. It gives us the politics of *kakos*, and the politicians thereof, who reflect what the people themselves love and are.

The ironic fact, however, is that a society which prizes and lusts after monetary wealth quickly destroys wealth, because it liquidates productive wealth in favor of negotiable and consumer-oriented wealth, money. It sells out the future in favor of the present.

A modest California ranch was happily sold by its owners in the late sixties for almost a million dollars. The sale meant travel, security, and no work to the sellers. The property worth a million in inflated paper, was actually producing a net of about 3% a year of its market value. Money in the bank, they reasoned, would do better.

By their sale, they sold out their son's future. After their capital gains tax, realtor's commission, and various penalties of an inflationary welfare economy, and after their year of travel, they had far less left than they had anticipated. Their capital was being diminished by inflation at a rate exceeding their dividends and interest. Moreover, by stepping outside the realm of production into consumption, they invited death, and the man soon passed away. Irrelevance always exacts a price, and the love of money is a love of irresponsible wealth, and hence irrelevance. Men and nations possessed by that love soon pass away.

# Chapter Nine

# The State as Thief

One of the built-in prescriptions for disaster is a misplaced trust. The motto on American coins, "In God We Trust," is an echo of an older Calvinistic faith, the belief in the depravity of man and hence a circumspect distrust of men and institutions.

Now distrust must not be confused with hatred. Thus, a sensible parent does not trust his nine-year-old son with the family car. He loves the child but distrusts his abilities. To distrust men and institutions (and ourselves) is to show a healthy awareness of man's sinfulness. It means placing our relationships and activities on a basis where all of us can work together without fear of one another.

Unhappily, however, without a sound faith, men will trust almost anything and anyone rather than God. Having denied God, men will then proceed to deify themselves, their own creations (including the state) and almost anything other than the living God (Rom. 1:18-23). Chief among these man-made idols or gods is the state. As St. Augustine pointed out, in *The City of God*, when men forsake God, and when a civil order becomes godless, it is soon no more than a larger band of thieves, a super-mafia, whose victims are the citizens. This evil situation is compounded by the fact that people insist on trusting this false god, the idol state. The more it oppresses them, the more they turn on state-created scapegoats, and each of them in turn becomes a scapegoat. But this is not all: to relieve themselves of a state-created oppression, they vote still greater powers to the state, crying in effect, "O Baal, hear us" and save us (1 Kings 18:26).

As we view the modern state, it is important to recognize one central fact: *the major enemy of the humanistic state is its own people.* The U.S.A. and the U.S.S.R. have their differences, and they may go to war, but both have been in continuous war against their own peoples from 1918 to the present. Savage as the treatment by the U.S.S.R. of Germany was, after World War II, it never equaled its savagery towards its own peoples. The U.S.A. has been generous to its enemies, and to all the world, except its own people. In the name of the public welfare, it has robbed, abused, and mistreated its own citizenry, and it is waging war against all segments of society, behind a façade of subsidies, and, with President Carter, began a war against Christianity as well.

People should have been forewarned. Early in the modern era, city planners, as soon as they came into existence, began to think of straight streets, not for the convenience of the public, but for the control of the people. An angry populace could be handled more easily by cannons shooting down straight streets, and rebellious peoples could be easily subdued by a cavalry charge up and down a straight street.

The *first* principle of the modern state is to protect itself against its own people, and to control them. Its *second* and lesser principle is to protect itself against foreign enemies. Foreign enemies are a periodic problem; the people are a state's permanent problem.

Thus, to entrust the state to control our lives, our families, our education, religion, and economics is to ask for our destruction.

The goal of state-controlled economics is the increase of statist powers, and the control of money is basic to that goal.

To trust the state with money is to ensure, virtually always in history, the debauchery of money.

Moreover, because the modern humanistic state is lawless, having denied God's law in favor of its own fiat law, any trust of the modern state is especially dangerous. It is like taking a vicious criminal out of a prison cell, placing him in bed with one's wife, and then walking away. The results are predictable. In such a situation, guilt lies not only with the criminal but with the husband as well. The modern state seeks total power by means of the control, among other things, of two key areas of life, education and economics. Statist control of either is a great moral evil. By controlling education, the state seeks to reshape the minds of future citizens into a predetermined mold. The increasing pattern of totalitarianism is power through control of education. Roland Huntsford, in *The New Totalitarianism*, has given us full documentation of this strategy and its use in Sweden. It is increasingly the totalitarian pattern. In the U.S., this same thrust is apparent in statist education, as I have shown in *The Messianic Character of American Education*, and in the growing persecution of Christian schools and churches.

The other area, economics, is under steadily increasing controls. These controls result in shortages, higher prices, inflation, a lowered standard of living, a loss of freedom and economic security, higher taxes, and much, much more. *Wealth and power* are transferred from the people to the state, and, as the state grows stronger, the people grow weaker and poorer, and they are enslaved.

Men, however, are voting themselves into slavery, because they are themselves slaves (John 8:34-36). Those who are by their self-indulgence and sin slaves by nature want the security of slavery in preference to the risks of freedom. Men cannot be free unless they are made free in Jesus Christ (John 8:36). Unhappily, all too many churchmen look to Jesus Christ, not for salvation and the freedom and the responsibility thereof, but for fire and life insurance protection. They have not known Him.

As we have pointed out, two key area of state control are education and economics. Let us narrow the second area. While all economic activity is somewhere controlled by the modern state, the key aspect of economics, and the starting point of all controls in economics, is the control of money.

Let us re-examine the history of money. The Greeks, in Lydia, are usually credited with inventing money and are said to have had a noble history of monetary restraint. The Greeks invented money *only* if we believe that money did not exist prior to state certification, and *only* if we believe that the state mints alone can make money. However, money existed long before the Greeks, and its authenticity was not a state stamp and certification but a just weight, a specific weight of gold and silver. Biblical law is emphatic on this as the required factor (Lev. 19:35-36); just weights refer to weights of gold and silver.

The Greeks thus began the debauchery of money by equating it with state certification rather than a just or honest weight of gold or silver. We are always told that, on the whole, the Greeks avoided debasing their currency or coinage. It was not for lack of trying! The Greeks, however, had a practical problem: they were a collection of city-states, not even equal in size to many American counties. Merchants quickly found themselves outside the boundaries of Athens or Corinth. It takes coercion to make bad money pass as good money, and the arms of a city-state were very short arms. The Greek city-states thus had a very practical restraint on their power to debase coinage, which an empire does not. Later on, Byzantium, while a large empire, had a continually variable frontier, losing and regaining vast territories regularly; it dared not endanger its usually precarious hold on various peoples by debauching its coinage. Hence, the fiscal decay of Byzantium was long postponed.

But, to return to certification: *certification is a guarantee, not of quality but of control.* A state certified and accredited school is not a good school but a controlled school. Nowadays, certification is an assurance usually of a debauched school. The same is true of money. All over the world today, virtually all state certified money is debauched money; it is not good but controlled money. Certification is the monetary (and educational) mark of the beast.

The medieval rulers of Europe were honest about the matter. They punished "counterfeiters" and coin clippers and openly held that all monetary debasement was a royal prerogative and monopoly. The situation has not changed since then, except that the state is less honest about its "right" to debase money.

How does debased money circulate? Gresham's law tells us that bad money drives out good money. Well before Gresham and Queen Elizabeth's day, Bishop Oresme had formulated the same principle. However, even then it was not new, Aristotle and Aristophanes having also made the same observation. Is it true? Does bad money drive out good money? Will worthless paper drive gold out of circulation?

Gresham's law is true, and *only* true, when bad money has certification as legal tender and state coercion behind it. Gresham's law thus presupposes a state monopoly and certification of money, not a free market therein. In a free situation, why should I prefer a paper $20, which now buys very little, to a gold $20, which now buys over 20 times as much as the paper does? It would be as logical as preferring a case of venereal disease to honest sex.

Of course, some will make that choice! In the 1960s, the Hippies echoed the ancient bravado of fools and idiots by declaring, "You're not a man until you've had the claps."

Do some people prefer bad money? Debtors, knaves, and statists do. Aristophanes, in *The Frogs*, has the chorus declare:

> I have often noticed that there are good and honest citizens in Athens, who are as old gold is to new money. The ancient coins are excellent in point of standard; they are assuredly the best of all moneys; they alone are well struck and give a pure ring; everywhere they obtain currency, both in Greece and in strange lands; yet we make no use of them and prefer those bad copper pieces quite recently issued and so wretchedly struck. Exactly in the same way

to we deal with our citizens. If we know them to be well-born, sober, brave, honest, adept in the exercises of the gymnasium and in the liberal arts, they are the butts of our contumely and we have a use for the petty rubbish, consisting of strangers, slaves and low-born folk not worth a whit more, mushrooms of yesterday, whom formerly Athens would not have even wanted as scapegoats.[1]

Despite Aristophanes' aristocratic perspective, his point is clear: bad people had by their political power triumphed, and they favored bad money because of its advantages to them. Hence bad money had behind it coercive, statist power, and hence appeal.

Thus, we can conclude, bad money is an aspect of bad morals and bad character. It drives out good money only when it is made legal tender, i.e., has coercive power behind it, in brief, when the state agrees to play thief on public demand. The state, then, in stages robs all those citizens who had earlier demanded the robbing of their rivals and enemies.

Bad or inflated money is always appealing to those who want money as wealth rather than non-monetary forms of wealth. As we have seen, non-monetary wealth means responsibility, and money allows for irresponsible wealth. In the modern world, limited liability has preceded inflation: it makes possible the rise of the corporation, and the separation of responsibility from monetary investments.[2]

Now, there is a limited amount of wealth as responsibility which we can safely and wisely assume. Beyond certain limits, non-monetary wealth will exceed our varying capabilities to handle responsibly. We can, however, assume control of billions of dollars in monetary wealth and be irresponsible. We then, of course, burn up the monetary wealth, as it were.

Of course, this is exactly what we do with our monetary system, when we use coercion to make bad money legal

---

1. Aristophanes, *The Eleven Comedies*, II (New York, NY: Tudor, reprint of 1912 London edition, The Athenian Society), 227.
2. See my works, *Politics of Guilt and Pity*, and *The Institutes of Biblical Law*, as well as *Law and Society*, for more on liability.

tender, certified money. We burn up the monetary system, and soon billions of dollars are as nothing.

If you have failed to get the point of all this, let us summarize it with the moral perspective all good works conclude with: certified education and certified money are bad. Do not put your children nor your economic future into the hands of bad men and bad money.

# Chapter Ten

# Money and Value

Men have often dreamed of a non-monetary society as a kind of golden age to be attained some day in the future. It is important therefore to understand both the problems of monetary wealth as well as the advantages of money.

Adam Smith gave us a vivid picture of English non-monetary society, before the rise of extensive commerce and a monetary market for produce. A feudal lord, having great assets in cattle and grain, then used most of it and marketed a limited proportion. Smith described the situation ably:

> Before the extension of commerce and manufactures in Europe, the hospitality of the rich and the great, from the sovereign down to the smallest baron, exceeded everything which in the present times we can easily form a notion of. Westminster hall was the dining-room of William Rufus, and might frequently, perhaps, not be too large for his company. It was reckoned a piece of magnificence in Thomas Becket, that he strawed the floor of this hall with clean hay or rushes in the season, in order that the knights and squires, who could not get seats, might not spoil their fine clothes when they sat down on the floor to eat their dinner. The great earl of Warwick is said to have entertained every day at his different manors, thirty

thousand people; and though the number here may have been exaggerated, it must, however, have been very great to admit of such exaggeration. A hospitality nearly of the same kind was exercised not many years ago in many different parts of the highlands of Scotland. It seems to be common in all nations to whom commerce and manufactures are little known. I have seen, says Doctor Pocock, an Arabian chief dine in the streets of a town where he had come to sell his cattle, and invite all passengers, even common beggars, to sit down with him and partake of his banquet.[1]

All this sounds very appealing. A bond was ostensibly established between the serfs and the lords. However, our modern industrial society created a greater and more far-reaching independence than anything feudal society knew. True, the interdependence is an impersonal and an economic one, but, under feudalism as now, a personal bond between higher and lower was made possible mainly by a Christian faith, not by any personalism inherent in the social structure.

Moreover, in the world in which an earl could feed 30,000 a day, any failure of crops, or other disasters, meant common famines. The lack of commerce and a monetary economy prevented the very ready and rapid flow of goods; even more, production was less geared to the market and more to subsistence. When money became an easy means of storing capital, and a ready measure of market-place values, trade flourished, and capitalization became easier.

Money provides a ready and necessary measure of economic values. Hard money, i.e., gold and silver, give men a convenient yardstick for economic activity. Just as a level and a measuring tape are basic to building construction, so sound money is basic to economic activity and development.

The problem develops when money, instead of being the measure of economic value and the means of the ready flow of

---

[1.] Adam Smith, *The Wealth of Nations* (New York, NY: The Modern Library edition, 1937), 385f. Hume's *History of England* is the source of the data concerning the Earl of Warwick.

economic goods, becomes itself value, not merely economic value, but absolute value.

Such a view of money has been all too common in history. Nero saw money as value, and, in terms of his virtue or strength, extravagance was required. Suetonius reported:

> He thought that there was no other way of enjoying riches and money than by riotous extravagance, declaring that only stingy and niggardly fellows kept a correct account of what they spent, while fine and genuinely magnificent gentlemen wasted and squandered. Nothing in his uncle Gaius (Caligula) so excited his envy and admiration as the fact that he had in so short a time run through the vast wealth which Tiberius had left him. Accordingly, he made presents and wasted money without stint. On Tiridates, though it would seem hardly within belief, he spent eight hundred thousand sesterces a day, and on his departure presented him with more than a hundred millions. He gave the lyre-player Menecrates and the gladiator Spiculus properties and residences equal to those of men who had celebrated triumphs. He enriched the money-faced usurer Paneros with estates in the country and in the city and had him placed at dice for four hundred thousand sesterces a point. He fished with a golden net drawn by cords woven of purple and scarlet threads. It is said that he never made a journey with less than a thousand carriages, his mules shod with silver and their drivers clad in wool Canusium, attended by a train of Mazaces and courier with bracelets and trappings.
>
> There was nothing however in which he was more ruinously prodigal than in building. He made a palace extending all the way from the Palatine to the Esquiline, which at first he called the House of Passages, but when it was burned shortly after its completion and rebuilt, the Golden House. Its size and splendor will be sufficiently indicated by the following details. Its vestibule was high enough to contain a colossal statue of the Emperor a hundred and twenty feet high. So large was this house that it had a triple colonnade a mile long. There was a lake in it too, like a sea, surrounded with buildings to represent cities, besides tracts of country, varied by tilled fields, vineyards, pastures and woods, with great numbers of wild

and domestic animals. In the rest of the house all parts
were overlaid with gold and adorned with jewels and
mother-of-pearl. There were dining-rooms with fretted
ceilings of ivory whose panels could turn and shower
down flowers and were fitted with pipes for sprinkling the
guests with perfumes. The main banquet hall was circular
and constantly revolved day and night, like the heavens.
He had baths supplied with sea water and sulphur water.
When the edifice was finished in this style and he
dedicated it, he deigned to say nothing more in the way of
approval than that he was at last beginning to be housed
like a human being.

He also began a pool, extending from Misenum to the lake
of Avernus, roofed over and enclosed in colonnades, into
which he planned to turn all the hot springs in every part
of Baiae. He likewise projected a canal to extend from
Avernus all the way to Ostia, to enable the journey to be
made by ship, yet not by sea: its length was to be a hundred
and sixty miles and its breadth sufficient to allow ships
with five banks of oars to pass each other. For the
execution of these projects he had given orders that the
prisoners all over the empire should be transported to
Italy, and that those who were convicted even of capital
crimes should be punished in no other way than by
sentence to this work.[2]

Not all who make over money into value are extravagant like
Nero; some are miserly, and others are thrifty. In any case,
money has become for them more than a yardstick or even a
storehouse of value: it has become value itself. The result is a
radical social disorientation. Men work, not to produce, nor to
gain properties, lands, and other assets, but for money. Money
then becomes a god; it becomes "the mammon of
unrighteousness" (Luke 16:9), the god of injustice, and the
logical goal of unbelief (Luke 16:7-8, 11, 13). Our Lord is
plainspoken: "Ye cannot serve God and mammon" (Matt.
6:24).

---

[2] Suetonius, *The Lives of the Twelve Caesars* (New York, NY: The Book
League of American edition, 1937), 259-261.

Money thus is very important, and necessary. But to make it the source of all value is a serious error and an evil. It leads in some, such as the libertarians, to absolutizing the marketplace, to making the free market and a monetary price the criterion of value per se. But money establishes economic value only.

Liberalism, by assessing life and man improperly and falsely, has contributed to the breakdown of both civilization and money. *First*, Darwinism and evolutionary thinking generally has reduced life to a struggle for survival and a conflict universe. The older liberalism, having a Christian hang-over, held to the harmony of interests, a view untenable after evolution was accepted. Money, then, became a weapon in this universe of conflict, not a means for achieving economic progress and harmony.

In a conflict universe, even the champions of the free market placed their emphasis on *competition* in a Darwinian sense. The emphasis was placed, not on the harmony produced by the free market and trade, but on trade as competition in the sense of war. Hollis noted:

> Liberal philosophy told man to devote his life to competing against his neighbors for the acquisition of material wealth. Then, very arbitrarily, it told him that in this competition he might use all means save those of physical force. But why should he stop at physical force? The only answer was that 'War does not pay.' But unfortunately this is by no means always true. A lot of wealth, it is true, is wasted in war. But on the other hand in war many people can be induced to work and to invent who would never do any such thing in peace. A lot of people lose money in war, but a lot of other people make it. It may be true that more lose than gain, but it is not possible to persuade the individual that he will not be clever enough to be one of the gainers rather than one of the losers. It is no more possible to banish war by an appeal merely to avarice than it is to banish betting by a demonstration that 'the bookie always wins in the end.'[3]

---

3. Christopher Hollis, *The Breakdown of Money* (London: Sheed & War, 1934), 95.

In the 1920s, many people held and taught that another World War was impossible, because it would be too devastating for men to contemplate as a possibility. Such talk was in evidence again after World War II.

*Second*, by its departure from Christian faith, liberalism, to a degree deliberately, and to a degree in spite of itself, has destroyed the long-standing supernatural foundation of value and made this world the source of value. Liberalism's hope was that man would be the source of value, but man, humanistic by nature because of the fall, wants himself and something more. That something more is easily summed up by money. Hence, the demand is for irresponsible monetary wealth, and inflation meets the demand.

The place of money in the realm of economics, as a means of economic activity and a measure of economic values, is very important, but when money becomes more than that, it is seriously misused and is also soon destroyed. Life is more than economics, and much more than money. Our Lord is clear on this point: "It is written, Man shall not live by bread alone, but by every word that proceedeth out of the mouth of God" (Matt. 4:4).

# Chapter Eleven

# Debt

Debt and inflation are almost synonymous. All inflation is a form of dishonest debt. Basically, inflation is an expansion of the money supply by the state. This expansion is essentially through the following means: *First*, the coinage is debased, and/or the paper money is increased and is without backing by gold or silver, or has fractional backing. *Second*, deficit financing uses funds exceeding the income of the state to increase the spending power of the state. *Third*, bond issues, or debts, likewise increase the money supply.

However, before a state or civil government can embark on an inflationary policy, i.e., on a way of life to which debt is basic, a population addicted to debt is necessary. If there is no excessive nor long-term debt, there is no inflation.

The Bible forbids long-term debt and limits debts to six years, and for serious reasons only. The seventh year must be a Sabbath unto the Lord, from debt, among other things (Deut. 15:1-6). As a general rule, we are to "Owe no man anything, but to love one another" (Rom. 13:8). God declares that debt is a form of slavery, and "the borrower is servant (literally, slave) to the lender" (Prov. 22:7).

In the modern world, however, debt is a way of life, for not only unbelievers but churchmen, and for churches and Christian organizations. Debt as a way of life has deep roots in sin, in pride, envy, "and covetousness, which is idolatry" (Col. 3:5; cf. Eph. 5:5; 1 Tim. 6:17). It is not only absurd but immoral for a debt-ridden people to complain about inflation and the federal debt. It is like hearing one devil complain about another devil's love of sin.

Because debt is so deeply rooted in sin and idolatry, debt, and its consequence, inflation, are especially morally and religiously destructive. An inflationary society is an immoral and degenerative society, and it will see, as its natural concomitant, every other kind of depravity flourish. No more than we can restrict a raging forest fire to bad trees, or to certain areas, can we restrict the scope of inflation and limit its influence to economics. Inflation affects more than economics, because debt has its roots in far more than economics.

Inflation and debt also affect the nature of power in a society. *First*, in an inflationary economy, it is not the thrifty, hard-working man who flourishes, but the debtor (at least, for the time). The moral foundations of society have been shifted to favor the worst element. In every area, as inflation is stepped up, the scum tends to rise to the top. The sympathies of society favor this degenerate element. *Second*, production gives way to consumption as the primary concern of the people. *Third*, there is thus a power shift in society, from godly men to ungodly men, from the thrifty to the thriftless. Spending becomes a personal and a political virtue. *Fourth*, the power to make or break the social order passes into the hands of debtors. General Lewis W. Walt (USMC, Ret.) has called attention to this most tellingly. When the U.S. Establishment (banks, civil government, etc.) has extended massive loans to states, firms, and organizations at home and abroad whose ability to repay is limited, then in time these borrowers control the Establishment and the United States. They can threaten to default on their loans and create economic disaster for the U.S. The response, then, is to give them even more! Thus, in the

1940s, Aramco sold oil to the Japanese at a lower rate than to the U.S. Navy, and American bankers supported the Panama Canal giveaway, hoping that its revenues might help Panama to repay them.[1]

The conclusion of all this is the destruction of the social order. Even those who see the immorality of long-term debt finally join the crowd, to exploit the opportunity, and destruction becomes their common lot.

It becomes apparent why Scripture takes so strong a position on debt: it is a moral and a religious issue. *First*, we have seen, debt is basic to inflation, and it is responsible, in all the moral compromise debt involves, for the immorality which marks an inflationary era. *Second*, we are forbidden as Christians to become slaves, and debt is slavery. "Ye are bought with a price: be not ye the servants (or, slaves) of men" (1 Cor. 7:23). *Third*, not only are we God's possession and property, and hence cannot become the slaves of men, but our time belongs to Him: we cannot mortgage our future to men by means of debt.

To live debt-free, except for emergency conditions, or a short-term (six-year) debt to pay for our house, farm, or business, means *to live providently*. It means weighing the moral considerations in every expenditure. It means also *to live content* with what we have; living in contentment is impossible if the goal of our living is consumption, things we want to possess, rather than in terms of glorifying God and enjoying Him forever.

Those of us who can recall the era prior to World War II can remember that debt was then very limited among most people, although business debts had begun much earlier to expand. Pietism had limited morality to the personal sphere, and hence moral men were readily immoral in the political and economic spheres. In the 1920s and 1930s young married couples did not go into debt readily, and their homes were largely unfurnished

---

1. General Lewis W. Walt, *The Eleventh Hour* (Ottowa, IL: Caroline House Publishers, 1979), 56.

as a matter of course. The idea of having everything at once was clearly not in favor.

However, the roots of our present crisis were present then. The churches had no concern with preaching or teaching the laws of Scripture relative to politics, economics, education, and much else. As a result, the churches helped rear a generation which is now actively destroying all the foundations of Christian civilization.

The word of Isaiah 8:20 still stands: "To the law and to the testimony: if they speak not according to this word, it is because there is no light in them."

# Chapter Twelve

# Economic Forecasting

Gary North often calls attention to his short-term errors in economic forecasting with a wry humor. This ability to err without loss of credibility or embarrassment, is a mark of the Christian economist. Why?

The Christian economist, working in terms of a Biblical faith and the knowledge that this is a universe of law, can work in the confidence that, within limits, forecasting is possible. Forecasting presupposes an orderly universe with predictable laws and movements. Thus, in order to have any kind of forecasting at all, whether in economics, physics, or other disciplines, either one of two conditions must prevail.

*First*, the totality of the universe must be the creation of a sovereign and absolutely governing and controlling God, whose over-all plan totally decrees all things that come to pass. This is, of course, precisely the claim of Scripture, that the living God so ordains and rules over all things.

Given such a universe, prediction is possible. The more we understand and study God's word and His creation, the better our apprehension of His laws, and the more accurate our forecasting. God, having perfect knowledge and total self-consciousness, gives us perfect forecasting. Beginning with His prediction to Adam (Gen. 2:17), God's word gives us one infallible prediction after another. Naturally, it is impossible for God to be anything but infallible: He made the universe, He made the laws and rules thereof, and He absolutely controls all things.

Forecasting in such a context gives us something to stand on, whether in economics or physics. Because we lack God's total knowledge and control, our forecasting can be neither complete nor infallible, but it has the possibility of reasonable accuracy. Thus, the Christian economist, knowing that he is not God, seeks to understand God's ways and to interpret them as accurately as possible. He can thus develop a body of knowledge and make more or less accurate forecasts. Because he is not God, he cannot comprehend or know all factors in a given situation, and thus his forecasting can be in error. However, because there is an inner consistency to these factors, the more he knows the more reasonably accurate his forecasting will be.

Some people, of course, are ready to turn on anyone whose forecasting is at any time in error. There is a great deal of switching from one economic forecasting service to another in terms of this. However, such an attitude is in essence humanism. It demands of man an accuracy and an infallibility which is impossible for man.

The *second* condition which *might* made forecasting possible is for man to control all the factors. This means totalitarianism: the economic planner becomes the god of society and issues a total plan of predestination for the economic order. If anything goes wrong, however, these humanistic gods do not confess to error: the plan is perfect, and therefore the fault lies with the people. Five-year plans do not fail because they are incompetent, but because the people are bourgeois, reactionary, capitalists, or else kulaks.

Thus, this type of economic forecasting rests on some fundamental errors: (a) It assumes that men are abstract pawns to be moved at will to conform to the preconceived plan. The people, however, may have other plans, or they may resent the planner's plan. In any case, the plan is in trouble because it treats people like chess-men, as abstractions to be moved at will but incapable of self-motivation.

Even more (b), God's plan is denied and left out of consideration. A politico-economic plan thus clashes with God's law and His eternal plan. The result is a failure, one circumscribed by, and a part of, God's eternal plan.

But this is not all. The humanist presupposes that forecasting requires controls, i.e., no controls, no forecasting. Outside of man, there is no plan, logic, nor meaning. Man must supply these things to society in order to make forecasting possible.

Now sound economic management requires forecasting. For a business or farming venture to prosper, there must be some kind of forecasting. Once man loses faith in the God of Scripture, he is in trouble economically, as well as religiously and morally. How can he make forecasts in a Darwinian world of chance? Capitalism, in the post-Darwin era, i.e., after 1860, began to seek humanistic intervention to provide the plan, in order to make forecasting possible. The result was the abandonment of the free market in favor of an alliance with the state. Since then, the major corporations, and minor ones as well, have often been very unhappy with federal planning and controls, but on the whole they have preferred their continuation in some form. Economic planning and forecasting by businessmen requires a plan: having denied God's plan, these men need the state's plan. They are thus closer to Karl Marx than to God. Marx and the modern businessman may disagree about the nature of his plan, but they are agreed that it must come from man, not God.

There is thus no real alternative for modern man. As long as he is a humanist, his choice is between variations of humanism: Marxism, Fabianism, Fascism, and the like, all humanistic plans. The consequences of his humanistic faith usually make him unhappy, but his unhappiness is better to him than the alternative, the living God.

Thus, the only tenable and reasonably accurate forecasting is of necessity on Biblical premises, on the presupposition of a God-ordered and governed universe. Classical economics, while usually Deistic rather than theistic, presupposed such a faith all the same and thus assured itself of intelligent forecasting. Increasingly, however, it is apparent that the logical alternatives are God and man, God's plan, or man's plan.

The forecasting of more than our economic welfare is thus at stake in our choice: our lives and eternal destinies are involved.

# Chapter Thirteen

# Why Humanism is Socialistic

How we define sin will determine the kind of people we are, and the kind of society we create. The Bible gives us a relatively short catalogue of sins: the summation thereof is in the Ten Commandments, and the details appear in various parts of a modestly sized book, the Bible. The Federal Government defines sin by means of a large library of laws, to which almost countless volumes are added annually. It is not Christianity which is a sin-ridden religion: it is humanism, and especially statist humanism.

Let us review some of the kinds of things humanistic man calls sin: it's a sin, someone has said, if you don't get the best possible education, or, provide the best possible education to every child in the world, every youth, and every adult. It's a sin not to do the best for your personal appearance: spend whatever is necessary for a good front, because "you deserve it." It's a sin not to be nice to everyone, even at the sacrifice of truth. It's a sin to be authoritarian about anything other than human rights.

Moreover, many hold it to be a sin to over-eat, or to eat junk food. Now, as an advocate of a Biblical diet, and as one who avoids junk foods, I can agree that a sound diet is a wise course, but is junk food really a sin? In the late 1960s, I had pointed out to me an actor, a homosexual, who loved junk foods but was emphatically a health-food man. His proneness to lapse into eating a few favored junk foods troubled his conscience, because he saw it as a sin in himself, and so spoke of it. He was indignant at any suggestion that homosexuality might be a sin, however.

The point should begin to be clear by now. We are prone to identify sin in terms of our standards, and what it does to us, not in terms of God's law. Scripture, however, tells us plainly that "sin is the transgression of the law" (1 John 3:4). God's law is eternal: it is also unchanging, so that we do not face a new definition of sin every time we turn around. (In 1920, racial integration was a sin to most humanists, a great evil; in 1950, racial segregation was the evil. Both positions are false.) Thus, we know where we stand morally as we face God, and what is required of us. With man, things are very different. This week, our foundation office received a notice going to all kinds of institutions, instituting a totally new regulation with a very severe penalty for failure to comply. Of the making of man's laws, and of new sins, there is no end. We have become a law-ridden world, with an ever-increasing catalog of sins.

Obeying God's law is the way of holiness. Obeying man's law is supposedly the way to self-realization. In reality, because there are no limits on man's law, there is nothing but suppression for man under humanistic law.

This is also true of non-statist humanism. Weekly, I encounter non-statist laws of sweeping variety. Today, a letter expressed a woman's moral faith: all men who wear beards are no good. Another: all churches are crooked, all preachers have their hands out for money. All coercion is evil. All appeals beyond man to the supernatural are evil, and so on and on. When men begin to make laws and to issue moral pronouncements, God's law looks very modest indeed!

Moreover, humanistic law changes no man. By its totalitarian scope, humanism does indeed finally make all things either illegal, immoral, or fattening, because man delights in total prescriptions. It is an aspect of his game of playing god.

One of the results of all this is that men go on sinning, but with a guilty conscience. It is said of Sweden that socialism has not abated the drunkenness thereof: it has only robbed drinking of its pleasures! As one junk food addict observed: I begin eating junk food because I like it, and then I over-eat because I feel guilty and want the comfort of the food.

Moreover, because of its self-absorption, humanists are given to dissecting and analyzing everything, including pleasure. If you laugh at any kind of humor, it is because you have latent hostilities. It becomes dangerous to laugh! (A woman, a militant liberal, turned savagely on a friend for "making" her laugh over a story which she decided was illiberal.)

In brief, socialism is a product of humanism, because humanism claims the right to legislate at will, and thereby to define sin at will. Because humanism extends its concern and legislation to every area of life and thought, it classifies more and more areas of human activity as sin.

In economics, it becomes a sin to succeed or to fail, to compete or to prevent competition. It becomes a sin to use our possessions under God; we must use them only at the state's will, if the state lets us keep them.

The Bible is a closed law book. No new laws can be added to it: it is fixed and permanent. Humanistic law, statist or anarchistic, is an open book totally subject to revision at the will of man. (Anarchists have, for example defined the coercion of the individual as the only sin, and they have also justified violence to gain their ends. The limits are variable in terms of their will, and thus there are no limits.)

There is no freedom for man apart from a closed law book. Where men can inflate the body of law, they can inflate anything. Economic inflation thus has moral roots. If men can make law, why not money? If men can redefine sin and lawlessness, why not economic laws?

Moreover, wherever and whenever men abandon God's law in favor of man's law, they have, among other things, opened the door to inflation. Instead of God's unchanging word ("Thus saith the LORD"), we have man's arrogant fiat ("Because I say so," or "It's the law" of the state).

Percy Greaves, with his usual incisiveness, stated the matter thus:

> Government, by definition is a monopoly of force. It represents the combined strength of the community in suppressing those things which the community opposes. In the long run, the government must always be popular. There is no such thing, in the long run, as an unpopular government. In the long run, we get the governments we deserve. No matter what those in political power may think, they cannot long do things that are not popular. We should remember this when we criticize some of those who are in office, because their powers to act are always limited by what the public is ready to accept.[1]

A civil government is thus a moral reflection of its people and society. It is moral irresponsibility to treat a civil government as morally responsible while we exempt ourselves and our society from the order the state has created. Our indifference to civil affairs, our unconcern with God's law, and our treatment of law as a thing to be made by man, are at the heart of civil dereliction. This is why God's judgment falls on such an order. This too is why, when the consequences of our moral failure begin to overwhelm us, God's word tells us, "And ye shall cry out in that day because of your king which you have chosen you (i.e., a ruler and a law other than the LORD); and the LORD will not hear you in that day" (1 Sam. 8:18).

The Lord will not hear us, if we refuse to conform ourselves to Him and to His law-word, to be His people. Then, we are told, "If my people, which are called by my name, shall humble themselves, and pray, and seek my face, and turn from

---

[1.] Percy Greaves, *Understanding the Dollar Crisis* (Belmont, Massachusetts: Western Islands, 1973), 108f. Greaves on these same pages gives an excellent statement as to why this is true of dictatorships also.

their wicked ways; then will I hear from heaven, and will forgive their sin, and will heal their land" (2 Chron. 7:14).

# Chapter Fourteen

# The Curse of Bad Religion

In a very telling article, "Farewell the Lollipop," James J. Kilpatrick attacked the federal regulation of food sales in public school lunch rooms. The new regulation would prohibit the sale of "junk" foods, or "foods of minimum nutritional value" until after the last lunch period. Kilpatrick was not defending "junk" foods: he was defending freedom. What is at stake is the issue of whether or not a central government can act *in loco parentis*, in the place of a parent, or, as the superior and true parent. "In a free society, we contend, the government is the servant and the people the masters. We reject the Orwellian nightmare of government as Big Brother, perpetually watching over our shoulders."[1]

From our perspective, in such regulations the state is doing more than act as a parent: it is playing god. In one area after another, the state is working to eliminate the possibility of sin, i.e., humanistic sin, by regulating and controlling man and society to try to make temptation impossible. What is in view is the society of Dostoyevsky's Grand Inquisitor. The Lord God made sin possible in the Garden of Eden. The modern

---

[1.] James J. Kilpatrick, "Farewell the Lollipop" in *Nation's Business*, vol. 67, no. 9. September, 1979, 16.

state seeks to make it impossible everywhere by regulating people into such narrow paths that nothing will be done except the will of the state. It seeks to eliminate sin by eliminating freedom.

In another very fine article, the economist, Thomas Sowell, deals with the mythology of prices, i.e., the assumption that high prices come from greed, whereas low prices are a result of virtue. Prices, he points out, are not determined by the arbitrary will of sellers but by the realities of the marketplace: cost, supply, and demand, etc. Supermarkets, he points out, make about ten cents on ten dollars worth of groceries. Insurance rates are determined by drivers; they are very high for Boston drivers because motorists in Boston drive with little morality and much damage. High rents in low-income neighborhoods are not a product of greed, but of high crime costs, vandalism, damages, deadbeats, and the like. He adds, "Perhaps the biggest reason why politicians want us to believe that prices are determined by greed is that they don't want the voters to blame them for the inflation that always follows in the wake of continued government deficits."[2]

Again we have here a religious problem: men love to believe that the evils of the world were caused by someone else and that they are the innocent victims. The more easily they can point a finger at a conspiracy (and conspiracies are real), or a profiteer, or anyone else, the more innocent they become in their own eyes. A man (incompetent, arrogant, and opinionated) who had laid waste his own and his wife's substantial inheritances was very vocal about rigged markets, and how he was cheated. (He himself was about as trustworthy as a three dollar bill!) It was a moral necessity for him to believe in his innocence and the evil of all who prospered.

Our problem is the curse of bad religion. Humanism gives us a religion in which either man or the state play god, and man, playing god, comes closer to being the devil himself.

---

2. Thomas Sowell, "Making Sense Out of Dollar Signs," in *The Los Angeles Herald Examiner*, Wednesday, September 19, 1979, A-17.

In a textbook for a college economics course, this religious nature of the new economics is plainly set forth. Ritter and Silber, the authors, begin Chapter 2 thus:

> The Bible begins with the creation of heaven and earth. Money and banking textbooks also begin with the creation – the creation of money by commercial banks. Creation *ex nihilo* is the favorite explanation in both cases. Unable to demonstrate the Biblical creation "out of nothing," we'll do the next best thing: Show how banks create money out of nothing. In order to see how it works, let's go into the banking business ourselves.[3]

This is an obvious fact, clearly and simply set forth by two very able men. This creation out of nothing, this playing god, is clearly recognized as such by virtually all, save the pietistic churchmen. Theirs is a faith in surrender and retreat. Christianity, or what they call Christianity, is limited to a small realm, called the spiritual realm. What such pietists forget is that, if even an atom is left outside the total government and word of God, man will use that area as an arena in which to play god. To limit the scope of Christianity is to limit God and to enthrone man as god in all the abandoned areas.

The Lord God has not abdicated any area of heaven and earth to man or to Satan, and for any man to limit the scope of God's government and word is to limit God.

Thus, at the root of all bad economics is bad religion, a false morality.

To re-establish sound economics requires therefore a return to a truly Biblical faith, to a belief in the sovereignty of God, the harmony of all interests in God's plan and decree, and to the faith that God's law governs every sphere of life and thought. Bad economics has behind it bad religion, and bad religion produces, among other evils, bad economics. We shall not deal with the root problem of inflation and economic distress until we turn to the whole law-word of God.

---

[3.] Lawrence S. Ritter, William L. Silber, *Principles of Money, Banking, and Financial Markets* (New York: Basic Books, 1974), 16.

# Chapter Fifteen

## Sin and Perfection

In a central sentence of the Sermon on the Mount, our Lord declares, "Be ye therefore perfect, even as your Father which is in heaven is perfect" (Matt. 5:48). The Greek word translated here as *perfect* means *mature, fully grown*, not, as the modern connotation would have it, sinless. The perfection of God is an absolute one, that of uncreated Being. Our perfection is to be different, a creaturely maturity. To be perfect in this sense requires growth, the process of sanctification. The Preamble to the U.S. Constitution uses *perfect* in this older sense: "a more perfect union" means a more mature union.

Now let us look at still another world, *sin*. In the Greek of the New Testament, we have two words for sin. *Anomia* means anti-law, iniquity, transgression, lawlessness; this is the sin of the sons of Adam; the redeemed man does not commit sin in this sense. The other word translated as sin is *harmartia*, meaning missing the mark, falling short. Christians do commit sin in this sense. The habitual practice of *harmartia* is, however, lawlessness, according to 1 John 3:4: "Whosoever commiteth sin (*harmartian*) transgresseth also the law (does transgression, *anomian*): for sin (*harmartia*) is the transgression of the law (or, is lawlessness, *anomian*)."

93

With this in mind, let us look again at the Garden of Eden, and at Adam and Eve. It was a sinless place, but emphatically not a perfect place. It was a place for work and growth. God ordained it to be the pilot project in the training of man to exercise dominion over all the earth (Gen. 1:26-28). Man began that task with nothing, stark naked. Of the many things he lacked on Day One, two were particularly conspicuous. Man had (1) no tools at all, and (2) no knowledge. Add to this (3) no experience, no history of previous human efforts to draw upon, and Adam's poverty in Paradise begins to emerge.

The Garden of Eden was orchards and garden, as well as wilderness. The animals were sinless also, but they were not perfect. The lion and the lamb may have been lying together every day, but, until Adam put up his first fences, they were lying on his vegetables, and eating them. Moreover, instead of rainfall, there was a very heavy dew which watered the earth (Gen. 2:5-6). On his first night in Eden, Adam knew that, while a well-fleeced lamb could sleep in that weather, he could not. Some kind of shelter became a necessity. He had a duty to dress and keep the Garden (Gen. 2:15), and this required tools, so his next task was tool-making. The fact that advanced tool-making as well as musical instruments appeared so quickly *after* the Fall (Gen. 4:20-22) indicates extensive experimentation in housing, toolmaking, and musical instruments in the era prior to the Fall.

Moreover, Adam had a scientific task, to name or classify all the animals (Gen. 2:19). To function successfully required knowledge. Adam obviously learned in due time which animals were best suited for domestic purposes, a fact in evidence after the Fall (Gen. 4:4, 20). Quite obviously, the Garden of Eden was a place of work, of trial and error, and of endless experimentation. We must recognize two factors in that work. *First,* man was not yet under the curse, so that frustration was not a part of his labors. It was precisely these frustrations that marred work after the Fall (Gen. 3:17-19). Work then was more difficult than now, because of the primitive state of Adam's tools, or experimentation with tools.

On the other hand, his work was productive: the curse did not yet mark all human efforts. *Second,* man's intelligence, not being affected by the fall and curse, had a greater efficiency and clarity of operation. This gave Adam a distinct advantage, but it still did not make up for the lack of technology.

The appearance or creation of Eve increased the work load. There was now an additional demand for goods and services. Clearly, Adam's original housing arrangement to avoid the nightly dew was not sufficient to meet the needs of two people. It had perhaps been no more than a lean-to, or simple covering; now, it had to be a home, something more than mere shelter. The presence of Eve aggravated the awareness of imperfections.

Enough has been said to make clear that, while Eden was sinless, it was emphatically imperfect, i.e., not a mature or fully developed environment. The remedy for that imperfection was, and is, growth in knowledge, technology, and work.

Satan offered a short-cut: they could be as God; it was God who was preventing them from realizing their full potential. Just as God by His fiat word, created heaven and earth in six days, so they too could create their ideal society by defying God's word in favor of their own creative word. The path of work meant subservience to God; it extended God's dominion, not man's. By asserting their own will and work, they could determine good and evil, and establish dominion for themselves, by their own fiat word (Gen. 3:1-5).

Sin thus entered the world when men sought a perfection in God-like terms, apart from God and in open violation of God's word. Man has ever since sought perfection, not in terms of godly faith and obedience, by work and growth in work, but by means of his own fiat legislation.

Keynsian, Marxist, and welfare economics give us clear-cut examples of this attempt to legislate perfection. Every economic system which seeks to gain full employment, economic redistribution, and an equal allocation of goods and services *by means of legislation* rather than godly work, and a free market for that work, gives us an illustration of this sinful quest for perfection without true growth. The only growth in such political and economic systems is a growth of statist power and tyranny, not a growth in human maturity. Instead of attaining growth, such a system destroys growth, so the result is sin, and no perfection as well.

Unhappily, all too many churchmen proclaim a gospel according to Satan; they offer a new Garden of Eden by means of statist fiats. They readily damn as heartless all who insist on the need for growth and work. They insist on the guilt of all who oppose their dream of a new Eden by statist legislation: they are seen as rich Christians in a hungry world, fattening themselves while the poor starve. Such caricatures abound: they are echoes of the tempter's caricature of God in Genesis 3:1-5. Meanwhile, the more they legislate paradise, the more clearly hell comes into focus. The debacle of all such efforts is very near. Unless the faithful know the moral meaning of inflation, and unless they recognize that man's fiats epitomize sin and imperfection rather than the way to Eden, they shall reap the whirlwind together with the many sons of Adam.

# Part Two

# Chapter One

# Economics
# and the Doctrine of Man

The word *totalitarianism* is a modern word for an ancient fact, for a condition virtually universal in antiquity and persistent throughout history. In the ancient world, ultimate power and authority were held to be immanent in the world of man, so that the arena of ultimate decision was always human history. The gods themselves were deified men who, as spirits, still were essentially concerned with the welfare of their earthly state. Thus, several Greek cities claimed to be the site of Zeus' death and grave, and Zeus, as a hero-king who was now a deified spirit, was oriented to time and politics. The gods themselves were subject to time and fate, so that their destinies were historically governed. Hence, their intense interest in history, and, supremely, in politics.

The gods were the gods of an historical state, city, or empire. Zeus was the god of the Greeks, Baalim were the gods of the Canaanites, Ra of the Egyptians, Dagon of the Philistines, and so on. A stateless god was held to be an impossibility, and the claims of Israel, that its God claimed lordship over all nations, indeed, all creation, was not believed: He was the God of Israel. The gods could be, like their state, imperialistic; like their states, they could be conquered and incorporated into the

99

conquering state. The gods were then included in the pantheon of gods as lesser and subject deities, as vassal powers.

If the gods could not be stateless, much less was it possible for man to be stateless. The environment and the life of man was held to be the state. Stateless man was a contradiction. Freedom meant total subservience to the state. What George Orwell depicts in *1984* was to a large degree, barring the technological refinements, normative in antiquity.

Because of this, religion in antiquity was a department of state whose function was to provide social cement to hold the state firmly together. Religion, then, as it again shows signs of becoming today, was *civil religion*, and the very word *liturgy* means simply, in its original Greek, *public work*. Religion was essentially civil more than personal; it was the state's department of public works designed to bind the state more firmly to the sovereign's will. Religion thus as an independent fact did not exist outside of Israel.

The same was true of everything else. There was, for example, no independent economic sphere, only the political control of economics. We are familiar with the fact that the word *economics* in Greek meant *household management,* but we are less familiar with the fact that the "house" was the state, and its economic life, and that of every citizen and home, was totally subject to statist management. A reading of Plutarch's *Lives* makes clear that citizens were simply an economic resource to be used by the state. In such a social order, people were more ready to be used, whether militarily or economically, because life *apart* from the state was to them the ultimate evil and life in the state man's only hope.

The exception to this totalitarianism was ancient Israel, and, after the division into two separate sides, Judea in particular. The office of priest was clearly separated from that of the monarch, and the prophet was the spokesman for God in applying the standard of God's law to a sinful social order. With the early Church and its world mission, this faith became a threat to the existing world orders. The result was the persecution everywhere of the Church as an enemy state and a rival empire. With respect to Rome, Francis Legge pointed out, "The officials of the Roman Empire in time of persecution sought to force the Christians to sacrifice, not only to heathen gods, but to the Genius of the Emperor and the Fortune of the City of Rome; and at all times the Christians' refusal was looked upon not as a religious but as a political offense...Whatever rivalry the Christian Church had to face in its infancy, it had none to fear from the deities of Olympus."[1]

By placing ultimacy in the triune God, Biblical faith removed it from the state. Neither the unity, particularly, nor the priority of things came from or was to be defined by the state. Their source was the ontological Trinity, which embodied the equal ultimacy of the one and the many.

The result was warfare between Christ and the Caesars and the destruction of the monolithic order of antiquity. In terms of Biblical law, the state is a very limited institution, hardly a state in the modern sense. Its taxing power is limited to a head or poll tax which is the same for all males 20 years of age and older. No other tax is legitimate. Basic to military defense is a citizen's army, with only a limited professional soldier possible in so limited a state.

It is not surprising, therefore, that while in Byzantium the Greek tradition survived enough to create a strong state, in the West the state collapsed, not only militarily but also intellectually. The civil organization of life was so radically altered that the population of Rome at one point was as low as 500, and urban life everywhere decayed. In a very real sense, civil government and economics became household management. The re-growth of urban life was largely made possible by Jewish merchants applying Biblical law to the management of trading centers, which developed into cities.[2] Europe gave promise of developing the integrity and freedom

---

1. Francis Legge, *Forerunners and Rivals of Christianity, from 330 B.C. to 330 A.D.*, vol. I (New Hyde Park: University Books, (1915) 1964), xxiv f.
2. See Irving A. Agus, *Urban-Civilization in Pre-Crusade Europe*, 2 vols. (New York: Yeshiva University Press, 1968).

of the various spheres, economics, education, politics, religion, etc. This development was frustrated, first, by neo-platonism, and second, by the revival of Aristotle's philosophy, and the result was the revival of the ancient totalitarian dream of a unitary order. Church and state were the main contenders for this exclusive role, with the university also asserting for a time a like claim. Once again the umbrella view of society prevailed, with church and state each claiming to be that umbrella under whose protection all men and institutions must reside.

With the Renaissance in particular, statist power and tyranny became once again prevalent. The Christian view of man as a sinner and a creature was replaced by the new view of man as ultimate, autonomous, and divine. Man now claimed priority, and the result was the destruction of the very limited freedom which had developed. If ultimate power resides in eternity, and the universe is its creation, there is then no competition, no "war of the gods" between God and man. Man's offense then is *sin*; while sin is an *offense* against the sovereign and eternal God, it is not a *threat* to Him. If ultimate power is transferred to history, then there is competition for ultimacy, a "war of the gods," and the freedom of man and of any sphere of thought or activity is a threat to all claimants to power.

The Reformation and Counter-Reformation for a time abated and altered the destruction of the integrity of spheres of thought and activity. Calvinism in particular began the development of concepts which led to a stress on the freedom of each sphere under God. Church, state, schools, economics, the sciences, the family, etc. are each independent and interdependent spheres directly under God, each with an obligation to serve God, and each without authority to rule over other spheres. The laws of economics were thus *not* derived from the ruler but from God. Accordingly, usury was not to be viewed in Greek terms but in Biblical terms, which meant that while charity had to be charity, and loans made in that spirit interest-free, all other interest was legitimate. The significance of this conclusion was great: economics was freed from Hellenic presuppositions and governed rather by God's law, *not by man*. The result was the progressive emancipation of economics from the state and its control. As a part of this transfer of economics from man's government, i.e., the state, to God's government, i.e., His law as revealed in Scripture, books began to appear to guide man in his economic activity. Such titles as the Christian navigator, merchant, apprentice, husbandman, etc., began to abound. The Bible became a handbook for business to an extent we cannot appreciate today, and the Book of Proverbs in particular was widely used, memorized, and cited by merchants as a guide to their actions. We have echoes of this reliance on Proverbs in Benjamin Franklin's sayings of Poor Richard.

The Enlightenment, however, was altering the philosophical framework of Western man and from Christianity to Deism, from revealed law to natural law. Government still existed beyond man, but it was essentially in Nature rather than in God. Whereas previously Christianity had declared nature to be fallen and hence not normative, Deism now affirmed Nature to be normative and the source of law. The rule of Providence now became the rule of natural law and laissez-faire. Laissez-faire is indeed a secularized version of the doctrine of Providence.

The kind of economic thought developed a few centuries earlier by Oresme now began to command the minds of men. *Nature* replaced God to a considerable extent as the source of all things and as the governing power. In Scotland, where older Calvinism still was strong, God and Nature were somehow tied together, so that the idea of the Invisible Hand was posited. The Invisible Hand is a theological concept; Nature was Newtonian and mechanical.

In any case, the result was a rapid development of economic thought and activity. Economics was no longer the household management of a ruler governing his realm but the natural outworkings of a law order basic to the nature of things. Freedom would in time produce the desired results and correct all evils.

The spheres were thus released from the umbrella of the state, and of the church. Whereas previously historical development meant the growth of statist power and order, or of ecclesiastical power and order, it now meant the growth of economic, scientific, educational, agricultural, and other activities and spheres. In fact, *progress* came to mean precisely growth in these areas.

The return of antiquity and its unitary concept of life in the state came with Hegel and Darwin. For Hegel, Reason, Nature, Mind, and Spirit had their incarnation in the state, and progress meant, not the freedom of the spheres and growth therein, but the comprehension of every area of life and thought in the state. Evolution for Hegel meant the development of the modern state. The foundations of such an approach had been laid by Kant; Hegel developed them, and modern socialism received its philosophical framework. Man was no longer God's creature but a product of cultural evolution and his future evolution best assured by the state and its power.

It was Charles Darwin, as Marx and Engels rightly saw, who gave socialism a measure of historical "inevitability." Darwin's work undercut the foundations of classical economics. *First*, Nature with Darwin ceased to be the arena or the glove of the Invisible Hand. Instead, Nature was depicted as mindless brute factuality, and man and the universe a product of chance development. *Second*, by this Darwin eliminated not only mind from Nature, but law as well. Evolution was seen, not as a product of law, but of chance variations. The universe has no inherent law, and the probability concept replaced the idea of natural law. Now the probability concept is itself under attack as too theological, because it posits some kind of inherent mind and order. The universe of Darwin is mindless and lawless: this is the *a priori* assumption of evolutionary thought in the main. *Third*, this meant that there was now *no basis* for classical economics. Nature has no inherent law, so that the free market can assure society of nothing other than the brutal survival of the fittest. Not even the fittest can be defined as other than the survivors. As Marx and Engels saw clearly, God had been abolished and denied earlier, and now Nature was reduced to a mindless brute factuality. Only one source of law remained: the State.

Earlier, Max Stirner had foreseen this outcome in Hegel's theory of cultural evolution, and he had set forth as the sole source of law: individual, anarchistic man, totally lawless and recognizing no law other than his own will. Marx recognized the logical force of Stirner's thought. Without God, and without natural law, only anarchistic man remains, Sadean man, and hence his long and violent attack on Stirner. Truth, Marx recognized, or logic, was on Stirner's side. Stirner's principle, however, dissolved the state and destroyed socialism. On pragmatic and religious grounds, i.e., as an article of faith, Marx asserted the necessity for socialism. There had to be state organization to remake man, to provide law until law became inherent in man's being.

The impact of Darwin can be seen in its logic, in the life of John Stuart Mill. Mill moved from classical economics to socialism, because for him the law basis of classical economics was gone. In the universe of Darwin, the only possible source of law is man alone, or man organized as the state.

Freud's doctrine of man further complicated the situation. How could Freudian man, organized or unorganized, be the source of law, when man is, in the depths of his being, ruled by the *id*, the pleasure principle? The *ego* for Freud is the reality principle, but also the will to death is incorporated in the *ego*, because the *ego* restrains the *id*, the will to live, by its recognition of the limits reality places upon our ability to realize the pleasure principle. Freud's man is irrational and lawless, and is essentially governed by a will to death.

The Behaviorist answer to this culminates in B.F. Skinner, whose research is well funded by federal grants. The vast majority of men are beyond freedom and dignity. Only a small elite miraculously rises above the inherent bondage of man. We are not told how, because this is an article of faith, that a few men are exceptions. This elite must totally govern, control, and condition all other men for their welfare and for society's survival. The survival of man requires that this elite become the law, holding ultimate power and authority. In such a perspective, economics again becomes the household management of a ruling class rather than an independent law sphere. The future of man and his economic activity is thus one of enslavement to an elite group of planners. As a teacher once affirmed vehemently to me, "In the modern world, freedom is obsolete" because it does not permit the controls which are basic to scientific experimentation. Society is increasingly viewed in Marxist and non-Marxist countries as an area of social science, i.e., of scientific planning and control. Here we have the abandonment of law for social experimentation. Instead of a *planned society*, i.e., one determined by an established plan, logic, purpose, or reason, we now have a *planning* society, one in which there is no pre-established plan or logic, but only endless experimentation. For Stalin, thus, as for all social experimenters, there were no *evil* acts in the mass liquidations, slave labor camps, and purges, but only experiments. Even unsuccessful experiments are scientifically valid, because they determine what can or cannot be done at the moment.

The modern doctrine of man has carried the pagan view to its logical conclusions. Not surprisingly, economics as a law-sphere is held in disrespect; what we have in its place is politics, or the political usurpation of economics.

Only as ultimacy is removed from man and the state and restored to the God of Scripture can we again free man and the spheres of life from totalitarianism. We are today at the logical conclusion of humanism and the age of the state. The decaying world order will not be renewed and reconstructed until man again acknowledges the ultimacy and sovereignty of the triune God.

# Chapter Two

# Manichaeanism, Law, and Economics

Law and economics are necessary aspects of man's daily life: it is impossible to live without them. The more a sound knowledge of law and economics decline in a society, the more radical will the decay of that society be. A decadent and dying society is one in which law and economics are in a state of radical decay or collapse. Together with theology, law and economics constitute the foundations of order in a society, and what men think of law and economics depends on their theology.

At the heart of our contemporary problem are false theologies and philosophies, and central among these is Manichaeanism. For Manichaeanism, the world is divided into two different and alien substances, spirit and matter. Each is equally ultimate, and both are self-sufficient and separate realms. To be spiritual in the Manichaean sense means to be disdainful about and unconcerned with material things, because they are alien and constitute a drag and a drain on the spirit. Spirit is held to be good, and matter, bad.

From the Biblical perspective, there are no two such different substances or beings (for in some dualistic religions there are two ultimate beings in and behind the two

107

substances). God is the maker of all things, and He created all things good. Because of the fall, all creation is equally fallen. "Spirit" and "matter" are alike fallen; they do not constitute two different kinds of substance or being. The distinction rather is between the uncreated Being of God and the created being of all things else. Salvation is not redemption from matter but from sin, the root of which is spiritual. Instead of despising matter, Biblical faith works to exercise dominion over the material world as God's appointed Kingdom.

The Bible is full of very precise and detailed laws governing the material world, the use of land, diet, wastes, wild life, and so on. When the Manichaean mentality approaches such laws, it finds them offensive. They are as a result ruled out, *first*, as a primitive form of religion for the supposedly primitive Old Testament Hebrews, and, *second*, as merely a secret code, with all kinds of symbolic meanings pointing to the truer and spiritual meaning, and rendering the literal meaning of the law as no more than a useless hull or shell.

The Manichaean influence on Western thought is profound, in both church circles and amongst the humanists. The Manichaean overtones, for example of Barthianism are very obvious in the division between faith and history, between holy history and actual history. Barth thus "affirmed" the Virgin Birth as a spiritual fact, but denied its historicity; Reinhold Niebuhr "affirmed" the bodily resurrection of Jesus Christ as a matter of faith but denied its historicity. For them, the world of faith must not be contaminated by the material world of history.

Law and economics are very material concerns, and basic to life. We are born into a law world, physical law, family law, church law, school law, civil law, and so on. We cannot escape from the law: *law is inseparable from life and is a condition of it.* Not even death affords an escape from law, in that, physically and religiously, we remain in God's universe of law.

The same is true of economics. From birth to death, our lives are economically oriented and involved, and every aspect of our lives involves economic considerations.

In fact, the progress of man requires the greater development, in terms of God's word, of law and economics. Attempts to eliminate law and economics from life, as in the Utopia of Marxism's ultimate goal, mean the progressive reduction of life to be a more and more beggarly status.

In view of this, it is an eloquent evidence of our Manichaean heritage that most students go through their entire schooling with no training in either law or economics. What economics they do get is really not economics as such, but a study of the political control and suppression of economics. It can be added that most lawyers leave law school with no training in the theology and philosophy of law.

But a true theology *requires* a study of law and economics. If theology takes seriously, *first*, the fact that God is the Creator, it will recognize the relevance of the material world and the centrality of law and economics. This it has not done. The United States, for example, has well over half its population listed as church members, and their ignorance of law and economics is perhaps equal to that of the unchurched. Such an ignorance is a practical denial of the doctrine of creation and a tacit affirmation of Manichaeanism. Law and economics have theological foundations which cannot be ignored. Our present crisis makes clear that law and economics decay without that basis.

*Second*, the Bible deals very specifically with law and economics, as I have pointed out in *The Institutes of Biblical Law*. It is impossible to deal seriously with Scripture without at the same time being confronted by law and economics.

The restoration of Christendom means thus a denial of Manichaeanism, implicit and explicit, and the development of a theology with Biblical roots. This requires a restoration of law and economics to a position of centrality in education and in human affairs. The rise of statism has been in large measure due to a theological default and withdrawal from the material world. To the redeemed man, the creation mandate to exercise dominion and to subdue the earth (Gen. 1:26-28), emphatically applies. This, under the guidance of Biblical theology, requires the study and application of law and economics.

# Chapter Three

## The Polytheism of the Modern Mind: Political and Economic Heresies in the Modern Age

In lectures delivered at Harvard in 1963 and published by the Harvard University Press, Clark Kerr, then president of the University of California, called attention to the change in the nature of the university. Kerr's work was a masterpiece of superficiality, and he himself was soon a victim of the brave new world of the university he proclaimed, as student riots dissolved the power of one administrator after another. All the same, Kerr's lectures called attention without a more than superficial awareness, to a significant fact: the university had become a multiversity. Even at Harvard, as far back as the late 1920s, only one-eighth of Harvard's total expenditure was devoted to what was traditionally regarded as the university. Things like Schools of Business and Schools of Journalism had become the major part of the university.[1] Moreover, something else had changed: the idea of the university as a unified field of knowledge and study had collapsed. We now have a multiversity. As a pragmatist, Kerr accepted this change without subjecting it to critical analysis. It is important for us to understand the meaning of this change from university to

---

[1.] Clark Kerr, *The Uses of the University* (Cambridge, Mass: Harvard University Press, 1963), 5.

multiversity, for implicit in it is the problem of a collapsing civilization.

The idea of a university is in origin Christian and Biblical. It is difficult for us, as the beneficiaries of twenty centuries, to appreciate the far-reaching implications of St. Paul's declaration of Ephesians 4:5-6:

> 5. One Lord, one faith, one baptism.
> 6. One God and Father of all, who is above all and through all, and in you all.

One Lord means one universe of law, one truth, one common body of knowledge, and one unchanging reality. It made possible the university, because it meant a common universe of truth for all. Although the collapse of classical culture meant the triumph of the barbarians, it was in barbarian Europe that the idea of the university took root and developed.

Classical polytheism could not offer a common body of truth because of its radical pessimism concerning reality. Because of the influence of Darwinism and the myths of evolution, we are accustomed to think of polytheism as a stage on the road to monotheism (and then atheism). Polytheism, however, is characteristic of the collapsed or collapsing cultures, not the young and growing ones. At the heart of polytheism is a denial of a universe, or of a common body of truth. Polytheism is the assertion that what we have is not a universe but a multiverse with a variety of options and realities. Truth and power changed as one crossed frontiers, or jurisdictions.

The mythologies of polytheism all give us accounts of the wars of the gods. Their philosophies all presupposed a cosmic conflict, the absence of any harmony of interests, and a radical conflict of interests. Polytheism in its every form sees conflict as a metaphysical fact, as basic to the nature of being, because no unifying power or God exists.

In a universe or multiverse of conflict, truth can only be extended by imperialism. Truth is pragmatic: it is real only insofar as it has power behind it. The Roman peace meant also the Roman truth and the Roman gods, all of whom were senate-created. This was behind Pilate's observation, "What is truth?" (John 18:38). For Jesus to speak of truth as something separate from, and above and over Roman power was incomprehensible to Pilate. In Aristotle's world view, his *Politics* determined his *Ethics*.

Polytheism is thus a symptom of cultural collapse, of the rise of relativism and a loss of meaning. It began in philosophy, with Descartes' principle, "I think, therefore I am," i.e., with autonomous man as the starting point of reality, and it concluded with the development in Kant through Sartre, which reduced the world of meaning to the mind of man. With every man as his own god and universe (Gen. 3:5), the only routes of unity between man and man became *love and coercion*. The bridge of an over-arching and transcendental meaning being gone, only a personal meaning remained. As a result, both love and coercion, or pacifism and war, have been major motives in the modern age. Man feels the need for a unifying meaning, and, since that meaning is not God-given but man-ordained, it is man who must extend it, by love or by coercion. In no other way can a single meaning exist in a meaningless world. Thus, polytheism, while seeing no common bond of meaning in the universe, feels the need for that common bond. The problem is, how to impose or create it, by love or by coercion? Eliminating the God of Scripture does not eliminate the need for a governing will and over-all plan and meaning. If we have no God to supply it, man or the state somehow must. The French Revolution began with high-sounding phrases about freedom, and it soon proceeded to a policy of terrorism unknown to the monarchy. At the time of the fall of the gironde, Robespierre prepared a private memorandum on the necessary course of a revolutionary regime:

> A single will is necessary. It must be either republican or royalist. If it is to be republican, there must be republican ministers, a republican press, republican deputies and a republican government. The internal danger comes from

the bourgeois; in order to defeat the bourgeois we must rally the people...It is necessary that the people should ally itself with the Convention and that the Convention must use the people. It is necessary to extend the present insurrection by degrees according to the same plan: to pay the *sansculottes* and keep them in the towns: to arm them, to inflame their anger and to enlighten them. It is necessary to exalt republican enthusiasm by every possible means.[2]

What Robespierre called for, *first*, was a *single will* in France. The unified will of the state replaced the unified will of God as the source of meaning. *Second*, to attain such a unified will, a totalitarian state was necessary. No other party could be allowed to exist in the state, nor an independent press. *Third*, the state's single will or plan had to be promoted among the people as well, and to gain this end the mobs were to be used to arm, to riot, and to exalt the will of the state.

In the present century, a like drive to totalitarianism marks virtually every modern state. Whether it be Marxism or the democracies, the movement towards the imperialistic coercion of all men is underway. The state is the unifying agency, and its single will must prevail, it is believed.

As against coercion, others present love, and, in the case of the libertarians, reason as the means of bridging the gap with some kind of unifying meaning. However, in a meaningless universe or multiverse, there is no reason to assume that love is better than hatred, or reason better than unreason, other than personal preferences. In an ocean of meaninglessness, neither love, reason, nor coercion have any meaning or value.

Besides love and/or reason and coercion, a third alternative is possible. This is a logical assumption of the fact of polytheism: it is the withdrawal to a private domain of private meaning as the only secure retreat in the sea of nothingness. In some forms today, this has meant Eastern religions and mysticisms, all alike given to a pessimistic world and life view,

---

2. Christopher Dawson, *The Gods of Revolution* (New York, NY: Minerva Press, (1972) 1975), 91.

often to the ultimacy of nothingness, and to a retreat which calls in essence for the care and nurture of the inner man in a collapsing world.

Such a retreat, unhappily, has marked vast segments of the Christian Church, including in particular the more conservative groups. The practical import of this movement is that these churches and churchmen, while affirming the God of Scripture, have reduced Him to one god among many: they have abandoned theism for polytheism in the name of Jesus Christ.

Of late, these polytheists have hailed a book by one of their number as the manifesto of their position, namely, Dr. Edward Norman's *Christianity and the World Order* (1979). This little work has been enjoying a remarkably favorable reception. In his column, Michael Novak, writing on "Religion and ethnicity are back (at last)," urges one and all to read and promote this work, and "Give it to your pastor." Haven Bradford Gow, in *The Christian News*, June 11, 1979, reviews it favorably. In the liberal *Reformed Journal*, July, 1979, Dale Vree does the same. The pietistic *Banner of Truth* (August-September, 1979) is delighted with Dr. Norman's conclusions, as is E.W. Trueman Dicken in the *New Oxford Review*, June, 1979. The *Encounter*, of South Africa, reprinted chapters of Norman's study as a special supplement in issue after issue.

Dr. Norman is no mean figure: he is Dean of Peterhouse and Lecturer on History at Cambridge University and has two works in history to his credit. *Christianity and the World Order* was delivered as the B.B.C. Reith Lecturers of 1978 and thus had a wide audience before publication.

What does Dr. Norman have to say? He begins with a delightfully telling critique of the Fifth Assembly of the World Council of Churches in 1975 at Nairobi. His analysis of "A New Commandment: Human Rights," is telling. He does admit that "biblical teachings have social consequences," but he is not interested in pursuing them.[3] Instead, he pursues the idea of "Christ's own sense of the worthlessness of all human values."[4]

Such a statement can be understood in two ways. *First,* we can assume that all humanistic or man-made values are invalid and therefore no ground for human action. In this case, we ground all our activities on God's word. We believe, then, that legitimate goals and values are tenable on earth, that God's law-word has a mandate for not only the Church, but also the school, the state, economics, the arts and sciences, and all things else. We then see all reality as God-ordained and created and of necessity to be governed and used in terms of God's Kingdom and law.

*Second,* we can reject time and history in favor of eternity in a neoplatonic assessment of natural reality as essentially meaningless or indifferent. We then approach all history with a "sense of historical relativism."[5] This is Norman's approach. For him, Christ's only word for history is "retribution and forgiveness."[6] Norman, who begins by attacking neo-Marxism in the churches, concludes by declaring that his historical relativism has some affinities with the Marxist view of historical materialism, "which also depends upon a realistic appraisal of the relationship between social fact and the adoption of ideology."[7] In other words, all our social action and our economic and political views are a class product. For Norman, God has no word for history, only an escape hatch from history. For Norman, the Christian-Marxist dialogue should have explored the social conditioning of politico-economic thought! In his own way, Norman calls for a surrender to Marxism!

---

[3.] Edward Norman, *Christianity and the World Order* (New York, NY: Oxford University Press, 1979), 74.
[4.] *Ibid.,* 82.
[5.] *Ibid.,* 83.
[6.] *Idem.*
[7.] *Ibid.,* 84.

For Norman, the church should show men the way to eternity. "Both in daily life and in the worship of the Church, the prevailing emphasis upon the transformation of the material world has robbed men of their bridge to eternity."[8]

Thus, Norman is an implicit polytheist, not a Christian theist. His god rules in eternity; history is left to other gods. We can agree with him only at our peril, because, behind his critique of the World Council of Churches, is a denial of the relevance of Biblical faith to history. His thinking ranges from neoplatonic to Manichaean implications. He gives us a religion which is very alien to the law and the prophets, and to the gospel as well. Instead of the triune God who is totally creator and Lord over heaven and earth, and whose law-word governs all things, we have an absentee god who enters history only to provide an escape hatch from it.

There is, then, no theologically valid difference between Marxism and a Mosaic economy. We should be indifferent to the politics of humanism and contemplate our navels and await eternity. Norman's god has no law-word for this world, nor any relationship to the God of Scripture.

Norman's heresy is by no means exceptional: it is a common one in our time, a product of a polytheistic retreat which masks itself as virtue. To say that our faith cannot be linked to the relativism of politics and economics is to say also that it cannot be linked at all to us, because we are, in all our being, a part of that same created world. We are creatures of dust, living in time, and we too should be therefore meaningless and beyond morality.

This is, of course, the point of Norman's critique. Politics and economics are illegitimate as religious and moral concerns. We have here the most radical form of Anabaptist thought, as well as a systematic antinomianism. His faith has room only for retribution and forgiveness in this world, and then an escape from it. He sees no creation mandate (Gen. 1:26-28) to exercise dominion over all things under God, no necessity to

---

8. *Idem.*

put every area of life and thought under the Kingship of Christ (1 Cor. 15:24-26), nor any sense of the relevancy of God's word for all of life. Those who advocate the imperialism of love, reason, or coercion have a more catholic or universal faith (at least in ambition) than does Norman, who is content with a very small god in a corner of the multiverse. He gives no faith for living, only a faith for dying.

Today, we face the death of the modern age and its faith. The death throes of humanistic statism, of the age of the state, are upon us, and this, the bloodiest of all ages in history, with a higher proportion of mankind slain than ever before by war, revolution, torture, famine, slave labor, mass murders, and the like,[9] is likely to see even more victims of the great Moloch or statism.

The great heresy is polytheism, which is the failure to recognize the cosmos as a law-order, a unity of meaning under God the Creator. Polytheism strips the world of meaning and leaves only an irrelevant personal meaning as the only ground for action. The consequences of such a demoralization of life and history are very much with us. In the dying, polytheistic Classical world of antiquity, only Christianity offered meaning and moral law to the world, as C.N. Cochrane, in *Christianity and Classical Culture*, has shown. Once again, in another perishing world of polytheism, the same faith alone offers hope. It has the word for every area of life. Economics is not simply a relativistic domain: it is a moral one, and it is the God of Scripture who says, "Thou shalt not steal" (Ex. 20:15). The differences between the various forms of economic thought are, among other things, moral differences having their roots in conflicting religious or world and life views. Law and authority are inescapably moral and religious concerns.

Norman's faith is a form of pietistic withdrawal from life and history and is thus far more radical in its departure from

---

[9.] Gil Elliot, *Twentieth Century Book of the Dead* (New York, NY: Charles Scribner's Sons, 1972).

the God of Scripture than the men he criticizes. Christianity has a duty to set forth God's word concerning world order.

# Chapter Four

# The Philosophy
# of Regulations

Ideas not only have consequences but they also have roots. They do not originate in a vacuum. Ideas and doctrines arise out of a realm of pre-theoretical presuppositions, which represent the basic and underlying faith of a culture. As a result, if we deal with ideas only, without delving into the presuppositions which give rise to them, we are then skimming the surface and neglecting the essentials of the problem.

Thus, in dealing with the philosophy of statist regulations, it is important to understand two separate things. *First*, there is the actual regulation, and the justification for it. Thus, city planning and zoning laws are passed in order to provide for what is called orderly growth and to prevent undesirable and anarchic consequences. This rationale seems highly logical *if* we begin with the presupposition that the alternative to statist planning is anarchy. Obviously, the answer is that city planning is necessary only when we begin with the presupposition that city planning and true order are to be equated. If for us order lies elsewhere, we will turn elsewhere. This means, *second*, that basic to any critique of planning is a philosophy of regulations or planning. Do we need a master plan, or planning, and, if so, where do we locate the center of planning, and who is the planner? Our concern here is with this second and more basic question.

Basic to any doctrine of regulations is a philosophy of order. What we believe to be ultimate order will determine our philosophy of regulations. It is important, therefore, to begin by glancing at one of the most influential books in world history, Plato's *Republic*. The influence of this book is, of course, not limited to classical antiquity. The Church, and Christendom generally, has through the centuries often and usually been more platonic than Biblical.

Plato's *Republic* is a blue-print for a planned and totally regulated society. But the blue-print is less important to us in our present context than the reason for it. Greek thought was, on the whole, dialectic. It believed that the world was made up of two alien substances held together only by dialectical tension. One of these substances was matter; the realm of matter is meaningless, lawless, and purposeless. As a result, the realm of matter can take shape only if the second substance, form, mind, pattern, or idea, was brought to bear upon it, to control and regulate it.

This view is, outside the Biblical faith, common to all of antiquity and most of history, although with variations. Thus, in Iranian thought, instead of two substances existing in dialectical tension, they are separate and in conflict. In the philosophies of India, the problems of dialectical tension led to a collapse into monism. The one substance, matter, was reduced to illusion, only mind is real, and the goal of mind is therefore an escape from the world of illusion. In a more extreme form, both mind and body were seen as illusions, and the result was a longing for escape from illusions into nothingness.

In the Western tradition, the dialectical version has predominated. In its first form, it was the dialectic of idea and matter; in the second, as H. Dooyeweerd has pointed out, it was the medieval dialectic of grace and nature. And, finally, in the modern form, freedom and nature. In the medieval form, grace collapsed and nature became the governing factor, and, in the modern view, freedom is becoming an illusion and nature the reality. Moreover, in the modern view, freedom really means the idea or plan of autonomous man.

With this in mind, Hellenic society becomes understandable. A handful of free men ruled over a large number of lesser men and slaves. The ratio could be ten ruled for one ruler, or much higher. The common people and slaves were part of the world of matter. The "free" men were men of ideas, men who represented the autonomy of mind from external and material conditions. They were, ideally, Socratic and ivory-tower thinkers, representing in purity the Idea or Pattern as devised by the mind of autonomous man. They were philosopher-kings whose duty it was to rule other men. Not surprisingly, the pupils of Plato were the Thirty Tyrants of Greece. Whether in Sparta or in Athens, the faith in the regulatory power and necessity of the Idea, Pattern, or Plan was basic. Human society, rational society, meant the rule of the Idea or Plan, and therefore of the planning men and thinkers, the men of ideas.

Critics of the early church have called it a collection of slaves and the dregs of society, a charge made repeatedly over the centuries. The church might have been stronger in some respects had this been so. In actuality, numerous bureaucrats, government officials, lawyers, and especially philosophers joined the new faith. They brought with them the form-matter dialectic and a belief in the necessity for the regulation of all things by means of the Idea. Throughout the medieval era, the attempt of men was to implement the rule of the Idea, either through the Holy Roman Empire, or through the papacy. While neither attempt can be reduced to pure Hellenism, all the same, Hellenism was basic to much of the struggle. Implicit in Platonism, and clearer in neoplatonism, was a faith in the purity of the Idea, Pattern, or Form. To the extent that man's mind separated itself into the life of reason or spirit, to that extent it partook of that purity. Aristotle had held to the

concept of the mind as a pure blank tablet, hence without sin
or prejudicial disposition. Thomas Aquinas made this concept
basic to his philosophy, as did John Locke later. This meant
that the man of reason, the philosopher-king, could, in an
ivory-tower kind of thinking, establish a plan of pure reason
which could best regulate mankind. The world of matter, the
physical world apart from mind, being an orderless and
meaningless world, regulation and control by ideas or reason
was seen as a necessity.

Not surprisingly, the renewed emphasis on Plato in the so-
called Renaissance (not so named until after the French
Revolution, c. 1815) led to a renewal of centralization and
control, to regulation by the tyrant states of the era. The world
of Bishop Oresme, whose theology led him to remove
regulation from man and place it in the nature of things, was
forgotten.

With Calvin, a limited measure of de-regulation set in.
Weber and others have over-stressed the extent of the practical
break, but understand the philosophical break. What Calvin
did was to remove the power of regulation from the realm of
mind and idea, and thus from philosopher-kings and place it in
God and God's law. His application was far from thorough,
but his principle placed regulatory law in God's hands, not
man's. The Puritan tradition in Britain developed this
implication. It was a racial implication, and only slowly
developed. It meant, simply, a trust in the Invisible Hand of
God rather than the visible hand of the state and its planners
as the true source of regulation.

It is ironic that this development climaxed in Adam Smith's
statement of the case for regulation by the Invisible Hand
precisely when belief in that Invisible Hand was collapsing.
Every other aspect of the 18$^{th}$ century doctrine of de-
regulation rested on the premise of the Invisible Hand, a belief
that the very nature of things was in conformity to the laws of
the Invisible Hand. The evangelical revival in Britain gave, in
the 19$^{th}$ century, a continuing vitality to that doctrine,
whereas, after Darwin, the collapse of the creationist faith led

to the search by churchmen for a new source of regulations, in the social conscience of the body public.

At this point, Marx and Engels were more perceptive than most men of their day. They immediately recognized the radical and basic contribution made by Darwin to their faith. Darwin had reduced the universe to a realm of chance, to brute and meaningless factuality. A *brute* fact is a meaningless, purposeless, mindless, and unintelligent fact. For Darwin, the universe is simply a vast collection of brute factuality. There is no mind or law in it, behind it, or beyond it.

This being the case, as Marx saw, there can be only one source of law and regulation, from the mind of man. For him the dialectical process provided the answer. The dictatorship of the proletariat is the infallible idea in history, bringing order to a world in disorder.

The inner logic of this position carried men into socialism. John Stuart Mill began as a libertarian and ended as a socialist. In this, he was more logical than later libertarians. Since there was no longer any ground in science for a belief in an Invisible Hand, a new source of order and regulation had to be posited. The logical source was the state. The Fabian Society was one consequence of such conclusions by the intellectuals of the day.

Since then, of course, men have been more persuaded of the brute nature of factuality. The universe is not only seen as mindless, but it is questioned as a unity. Clark Kerr held that we have in reality a multiverse, and the university thus had to become a multiversity. The older concept of the university was a uniquely Christian concept and a product of Christendom. It rested on the premise of one God, one law, one universe of truth and meaning. Now the idea of good and evil, right and wrong was denied. The doctrine of absolute truth and a universe of total meaning was dismissed. This has meant that the new realm of meaning is man, and therefore man's agency, the state. Absoluteness, having been denied to God and His truth, was transferred to the state, and the result is totalitarianism. The attributes of God have become the attributes of the modern state. The Idea governs and regulates absolutely, and its name is statist man.

Until truth and law are again located in the sovereign God of Scripture, and all regulation and predestination ascribed to God and His laws for men, until then we will continue to have the totalitarian regulatory state. We will have predestination by state planners, and cradle to grave, or womb to tomb, government by the new hand of "providence," a statist agency. Men act out their faith in history, and historical problems are enactments of faulty and erroneous faiths. To clean up a society, we must clean up its presuppositions. This, clearly, is a religious task.

# Chapter Five

# The Doctrine of the Harmony of Interests

Ludwig von Mises has called attention to the importance of the doctrine of a harmony of interests to the free market and its economy.[1] It is necessary for a Christian to recognize how basic this concept is to a Biblical world and life view as well. Even more, we must hold that only in terms of Biblical presuppositions is it possible to declare that a harmony of interests rather than a conflict describes reality.

The concept of a harmony of interests rests on the Biblical doctrine of creation. God having made all things by His fiat word, all things move from all eternity in terms of His eternal decree (Acts 15:18; Prov. 16:4; Gen. 1:31; Acts 17:24; Col. 1:16; Ex. 20:11, etc.). Thus, metaphysically, the universe is a unity, moving in terms of an absolute and predetermined harmony. Sin and evil are *moral or ethical* facts or states, not *metaphysical*, and, even as moral facts, serve God's absolute harmony of purpose and interest: "I am the LORD, and there is none else. I form the light, and create darkness: I make peace, and create evil: I the LORD do all these things" (Isa. 45:6-7). "The Lord hath made all things for himself: yea, even the wicked for the

---

1. Ludwig von Mises, *Human Action* (New Haven, Conn.: Yale University Press, 1949), 660-684.

day of evil" (Prov. 16:4). The consequences of this doctrine are far-reaching. It is a declaration that even the most flagrant cases of evil have totally governing them an absolute harmony of interests. Thus, at the moment of history's supreme evil, the planned injustice of the trial and death of Jesus Christ, St. John tells us that here the eternal counsel and glorious purpose of the Father was fully set forth (John 11:47-53).

Among the covenant peoples, both before and after Christ, this doctrine was commonly by-passed. The common pagan world and life views of antiquity, and that of Hellenic philosophy, prevailed. It was held rather that a radical conflict of interests prevails. In mythology, this conflict was pictured as polytheism and the wars of the gods. Instead of a universe, a polyverse was assumed to exist, with varying forces in the ascendancy. In the Orient, this meant the yang and the yin philosophy; in the West, it meant the concept of the wheel of fortune. In any case, it meant that man faces a world of metaphysical and inescapable conflict.

But man needs *harmony*. For civilization to advance, harmony is an essential. The more radical the views of conflict, the more likely it is that the culture will be nomadic and incapable of maintaining a sustained settlement and growth. How, in the metaphysics of ultimate conflicts of interest, was any civilization possible? Mythology provided an answer: the gods from time to time attained a temporary peace by means of divine imperialism. Zeus supplanted his father and ruled over his rivals, although not without conflicts. Similarly, imperial man could establish a tenuous and temporary peace by means of imperialism. In the East, this meant Oriental despotism; in the West, it meant Plato's *Republic*, a totalitarian state. Man imposes a man-made, statist harmony of interests as the only means of controlling the metaphysical conflict of interests.

The Biblical presupposition is that metaphysical harmony of interests predetermines and uses every ethical conflict of interests to effect an ultimate harmony. Every non-Biblical view presupposes a metaphysical conflict of interests and sees the solution in moral man's ethical predetermination and imposition of a statist harmony of interests. The Bible declares evil to be a moral fact in man; non-Biblical views see evil as a metaphysical fact in the universe which can only be subdued by the moral actions of a civil state.

Unhappily, during most of Christian history, syncretistic ideas have compromised Biblical faith and allowed an extensive faith in the pagan concept of conflict to prevail. All the same, only within the context of Christian civilization has the doctrine of harmony prevailed to any degree. Evidence of this success, albeit a limited one, can be seen in the fact that, outside of Christendom, totalitarianism can be seen as an inevitable and necessary fact, whereas within, it has been seen as a common and too prevalent evil.

With the rise of Darwinism and evolutionary thought, pagan concepts of conflict have once again captured not only society at large but most of the churches. Conflict is presupposed as basic to being in the social pronouncements of many churches, and the solution is seen as moral action by the welfare state. The benevolent and omnipotent God of Scripture is increasingly being replaced by the benevolent and omnipotent state.

Thus, the modern, humanistic world and life view is marked by certain presuppositions which are radically at odds with Biblical faith. *First*, the universe is seen, not as the planned and predestined work of the sovereign and triune God of Scripture, but as the product of an evolution which is solely the work of chance.

*Second*, in this world of chance, there is a struggle for survival, and the result is the survival of the fittest. A radical disharmony and conflict of interests is thus presupposed. The survivors continue at the expense of others, and nature is red in tooth and claw.

*Third*, this perspective has led to two seemingly diverse perspectives, the extremes of "rugged individualism" or "predatory capitalism" so-called, and of socialism. Both, however, are agreed that conflict is the basic fact of life. The social Darwinian who affirms "rugged individualism" is content with this fact of conflict. The socialist, while agreeing with this faith in conflict, is unhappy because of it. In reality, the two groups have been allies in the 20th century, and most corporations and industries are fearful of the free market, seek subsidies, and demand a working alliance with the interventionist state. Disagreements between capital, labor, and civil agencies are thus family quarrels between members of an interventionist tribe. All presuppose conflict as basic to reality and seek a man-made solution; they differ as to which set of men and ideas can best provide the controlling harmony.

*Fourth*, evolutionary thought repeals the past and thereby outlaws economics as an independent discipline. In an evolving universe, no predetermined law, pattern, or goal can exist. *Change and chance* govern all things, which means that past experience cannot predicate nor predict the future. In an evolving reality, Durkheim held, there can be no law derived from the universe, no moral or immoral standards, and no normal and abnormal facts. The criminal can thus be a social pioneer.[2] The state, therefore, cannot be criticized when it embarks on a program of controls because, if for no other reason, there are no values whereby any judgment can be made. There are only scientific experiments in social planning; in the U.S.S.R., whatever loss of life, production, or resources a plan may cause will be regarded as merely a failed experiment, not as an evil thing.

*Fifth*, this means that values, if they exist at all, must be man-made. Because the universe is merely change and chance, values *cannot be derived* from the nature of reality, but must be *imposed upon* it by man. The state, as man's agency, or, in anarchism, man alone, creates the value out of nothing and then imposes it upon reality. God's fiat will is replaced by the fiat will of man or the state. Since every man's fiat will is equally valid, the result is a contest of wills, and the state's will

---

2. Emile Durkheim, *The Rules of Sociological Method* (New York, NY: The Free Press, (1895) 1966), 66ff.

is the winner. There is, then, no ground for a moral condemnation of the state's will. The individual's fiat will has no moral validity outside of his being. In a conflict-of-interests universe, the fiat will with the greatest power prevails, morally and existentially.

*Sixth,* one consequence of this prevailing power of the state is its control of education as a means of perpetuating its fiat will. To maintain its control over the body politic and over the market-place, the state controls education as well. Statist education takes a cynical attitude towards Christianity, economics, morality, and all things else, save the scientific socialist state.

*Seventh,* the Darwinian perspective, as well with all evolutionary faiths, holds to an open universe, i.e., a universe which is evolving and is open to all kinds of potentiality other than whatever Scripture declares. In a world of unlimited possibilities, man must control evolution, which means practically, that the scientific socialist state must control man and history. Statist evolution presupposes the repeal of the past and the control and determination of the future by the scientific socialist state. Education can thus disregard history and law because in an open universe all things are determined by present planning and controls.

*Eighth,* this means that the key to the future is in statist controls. Economics thus means controls, not freedom. A school teacher in the 1960s charged me with quackery for speaking of freedom. She declared, "In the modern world, freedom is obsolete." For her, in a world of change and chance, order and progress require the scientific control of society by the state, and freedom becomes an antiquated and disruptive notion. Her thinking was logical, but her antichristian presupposition false.

*Ninth,* with this rejection of freedom comes a trust in the state and its powers. We have seen in this century a swing from a belief in unlimited natural resources to a rigid belief in very limited natural resources. Both views are false and dehumanizing. To believe in unlimited natural resources is to presuppose an infinite universe of materials; thinking, choice, and development are then reduced to a minimum. In an age-old myth, it has been held that, in a true wilderness as yet uncontaminated by man, man can live easily and readily off of nature's supposed bounty. No such condition has ever existed. Wilderness areas provide the most meager existence and require man's beneficent exploitation to become productive. On the other hand, to believe in very limited resources, as is common today, means that the state must nurse, control, and carefully ration all resources. Neither of these pagan views does justice to the God-created nature of things. In terms of a Biblical perspective, the universe is not infinite: it is created and limited. Man too is a creature, and limited. But man, created in God's image, is confronted on all sides with a limited but still vast world of potentiality which his free work and intelligence can utilize towards exercising dominion and subduing the earth (Gen. 1:26-28). The key factor, then, is not the unlimited or limited nature of resources, but the moral freedom of man to develop himself and the world around him.

Man must be free first of all from his own sin and guilt and then also from the state which plays god over him. Man the sinner is in bondage to sin in himself, and only Christ can give him true freedom (John 8:31-36). Sin is slavery, and man in sin seeks slavery in all things and creates an enslaving state by means of his demands for cradle-to-grave security. Seeing the world as a conflict of interests because he himself is in conflict with God, and then with his fellow-man and himself, man looks to escape from that conflict by creating a great idol to which he renders homage, the modern state. This god-state becomes his safe harbor and refuge from the storms of conflict. The conflict only increases, however, because man the sinner and his idol-state are at war with harmony. They are in the business of manufacturing conflict wholesale and then crying wolf over it. The harmony they seek requires the death of God, an impossible fact. The economics of conflict thus breeds conflict and feeds on itself. The state, as the agency for stilling conflict and producing harmony, becomes a perpetual conflict machine, providing endless justification for its role as the peace-maker.

The state's capacity for self-justification becomes amazing. Thus, in the Soviet Union, a state created supposedly to end "feudalism" and "economic slavery," political prisoners are bought and sold as slave workers by the wagonloads by district bosses.[3]

From all of this, there can be no return except by a return to Biblical faith. Only the God of Scripture gives us a universe with a harmony of interests. The alternatives to that world all point in the direction of the Soviet slave labor camps and worse. No religion, economics, politics, or education can do other than destroy man if it abandons the God of Scripture.

---

[3.] Alexsandr I. Solzhenitsyn, *The Gulag Archipelago, 1918-1956,* vol. III (New York, NY: Harper & Row, 1978), 395.

# Part Three

# Appendix

# Money, Inheritance, and the Family
## By Elizabeth McEachern Miller

What I would like to do is put our inflation and monetary problems in an historical framework. Although many of us have just awakened to the magnitude of the global crisis we face, I would like to try to show that it has not been either accidental or a series of foolish blunders by our leaders in Washington, D.C. which has led us to this place. It has actually been a gradual transition or change of ideas about property and wealth which has been developing in our country for a long time, and we are just now beginning to bear its terrible consequences. What originally seemed to be the rantings of second-rate professors and intellectual ne'er-do-wells has come to pass and borne ill fruit in our generation.

We have come to a crossroads in our history. The choice made will be an individual one, but will have collective results.

The catalyst that is forcing us to choose a direction is the same that is enrolling us into conferences of this nature: our property system is under attack.

Basically, modern man has existed under one of two property systems, either state ownership and control, or private ownership.

In our day we have several representative systems of state ownership. Communism, as practiced in the USSR, is the most advanced. However, total centralized power is suicidal, and starvation would bring down the system, so certain "sneaky" concessions are made to the farmers. They are allowed to raise produce on small plots to be sold privately in local markets. This little tolerated freedom, plus many unpublicized deals with our government, keeps the system operating and the Russian people alive.

Swedish socialism, although in appearance more benevolent, is as deadly to the soul as communism to the body, and the nation is committing suicide with alcohol.

We are seeing the British nation barely fend off complete collapse as the ideas of Fabian socialism have strangled that once vibrant people.

Benito Mussolini should be given credit for the particular brand of statism that has found such a fertile environment in our own country. His system was not one of direct take-over through revolution, but gradual ownership through regulations and controls. The velvet noose is slowly choking off our productive capacity, restricting our freedom of movement, and swamping us in a sea of paperwork.

Under our increasingly controlled economy, the state becomes a giant umbrella under which each sphere of our lives is regulated. Our property can only be used in certain ways. Our educational systems must be in tune with H.E.W. official dogma. Our business and professional lives are always adjusting to more encroachments on our freedom to exercise our own judgments. Under a statist property system, nothing is allowed to exist outside of, or independent of the big umbrella of central planning.

When everything in our country is planned and run like our postal system, we will have arrived by degrees into this cradle-to-grave security system whereby we are relieved of the responsibility of making any decisions, but also of the "privilege" of eating or, at least, of eating well.

To finance the "big umbrella" that covers our lives requires a tax, and the most efficient arm of this property control system is always the collecting arm. The spending side of government is loose, corrupt, and inefficient, but the extracting side always works well, because it is the life blood of the system.

This is the direction into which we are moving. Pick any area: medical, dental, church, real estate, travel, personal privacy, and the sphere of operating freedom is lessening like a closing vise.

We find ourselves at this juncture. My argument is that basically we have arrived at this point because we wanted to be here. We asked for this, and we got it. I am not saying we like it, but I am saying that we voted for it and are still voting for it. We are not a captive nation, and this system has not been imposed upon us by foreigners. It is of our own making, and although certain aspects of the big umbrella system have become uncomfortable, I am not sure that the discomfort has been enough to impel us to get this statist monkey off our back.

There is another property system which I will call the "total free enterprise view." This theoretical position is held by Libertarians and some conservatives. The writings of Ayn Rand have done much to propagate this viewpoint. It asserts that ownership of wealth and property is exclusively personal. Man is limited in his acquisitions and dispersal of his property solely by the market place. In this "survival of the fittest" system of ownership, pornographic endeavors, drug dealings, and other such activities become legitimate. If it sells, it is valid.

This anarchical view of wealth appeals to our greed and is dangerous because it wars against the existing governmental system, but offers no replacement. As an example, these freedom-loving anarchists were widespread in Russia before the revolution of 1917. It was their unrealistic, utopian proposals that helped topple the existing monarchy of Nicholas II; but it was the organized cadre of Bolsheviks who took control and put to death their freedom-loving brothers. It was this anarchistic element of freedom and love that viewed the state as slowly withering away. In this century there is no state that is withering. Government systems do not wither, they are usurped, usually by foreign states, or their power is usurped from within by local seats of power, of which the family could very definitely be one.

To conclude this discussion of the private and personal view of wealth as put forth by certain free enterprise elements, it is necessary that I show a psychological side-effect that this position creates. Personal ownership of wealth is a responsibility, and when property is held exclusively by an individual with only the marketplace as a source of direction, then this responsibility can become a great burden to modern man. It is under this view of property that guilt imposes its unbearable weight and ownership or heirship becomes a curse.

To get out from underneath this burden of guilt, man looks for and finds all kinds of legitimate and illegitimate ways to remove the responsibility of ownership and its attendant guilt from off his shoulders. My time permits only two examples. One is gambling. Whenever you see gambling become a popular past-time, you can be assured that it is the means used to remove wealth and its responsibility from the shoulders of the possessors. Studies show that men and women gamble to lose and return to their homes and businesses refreshed and renewed.

My other example is more to the point of this conference. Statism, as a governmental system, acts in much the same way as a gambling casino. It is the vehicle used to remove the responsibility of wealth from the shoulders of those not prepared to bear it. Remember, as I said before, we are still voting for this system. Our citizens do not want wealth or property about which they must make decisions. They want to play, like children, in public parks or sport palaces.

Our foreign policy also shows that we cannot bear the burden of world leadership and power, and we are committing national suicide by throwing our inherited wealth at every country in the world. It is now estimated that we are paying Panama upwards of $4 billion to take the Canal off our hands.

To recapitulate: First, statism, as a property system is destructive to freedom, to capital and wealth. Society decays materially and spiritually whenever or wherever it is adopted.

Second, anarchy, or total free enterprise, is only a theory, although practiced to some degree within a property system which allows moral and entrepreneurial freedom. This system breeds envy, guilt, and class consciousness. It is a dangerous position, because many people today believe that this is what we fought the American Revolution over. This is not true.

The third view of property has a long history and is familiar to all of us. This view is the Biblical system which owns and holds property within the family unit. This is the view of property set fort by our American forefathers, and our government charter. The Constitution embodies this view. Basically, it is this position which is under attack today. This family system of ownership needs to be thoroughly re-examined and re-thought among economists, educators and businessmen in order to re-establish a system which will have the strength and unity to withstand the "inevitable" rising tide of socialism. Here, in the United States, we have had this Biblical property system in operation to a greater degree than is generally known or admitted today. Our law structure, which supports this property system, is founded on the Decalogue or Ten Commandments. "Thou shalt not steal," does not permit our government to rob us of our income through taxes or inflation. Also, it does not allow the central government to assume itself to be the ultimate owner of our land, allowing us to rent it for an ever growing fee called property taxes. "The earth is the Lord's," and the ultimate owner is God, the Creator, who created it for man to use in certain ways. "Government" is also ordained of God, but not as the owner of all property. It has another function.

Today, many people are concerned about the "break-down of law and order": and it is important to be perfectly clear about what is taking place. This country is not having a break-down of law, in the sense that there is less law now. As we all know, we have an increase of laws. What we are witnessing is the gradual transition from our Biblically-based law and property system to an arbitrary statist law system. This new law system is based on the desires of the social, central planners in Washington, D.C. The edicts of H.E.W., of the Treasury Dept., the State Dept., or I.R.S. will replace our old system, and ownership and wealth will be denied or allowed by the current elite in control.

Not only did we have, formerly, a Biblical or family ownership system of wealth, but it was supported by its own law structure. This property view takes its authority from Scripture, where the earth and all its resources are made for man's use by his Creator, and he holds all his wealth and possessions in trust. He is required to add to it (capitalization), tax himself out of the increase, and to distribute his estate to the next generation through the family.

There are many ramifications of this property system which I do not have the time to explore with you, but I would like to mention one area in particular: the tax structure.

Under the Biblical system, which was re-established, in part, by the Puritans in this country, there were essentially two taxes. The first was a "head tax," which was uniform for all citizens; therefore, it had to be small enough for the poorest to pay.

Because the central government was considered to be only a ministry of justice, its function was limited to the punishment of evil doers. Therefore this small "head tax" supported the court system, plus the needed military expenses.

The other required tax, the tithe, was limited to 10% and it was to be paid out of one's increase or income. All the major social functions of the culture are to be maintained by this tax. It is important to note this point. The head tax is the support of the civil order, and the tithe, the support of the social order, and its use as directed by the tither or producer. Education, welfare, the church and more are the recipients of this tax. This producer-directed-giving principle of government impressed Alexis de Tocqueville when he visited this country in 1831. The statist European system stood in stark contrast to the almost invisible government of the United States, with all its widespread principle of private giving, taking care of all the social ills of the communities.

As you can readily see, this tax system alone would make for a strong people and a weak bureaucracy.

Historically speaking, this country began with a property system which was Biblical. Because of this foundation and its law structure, wealth increased almost miraculously, or so it seemed to visitors from the old world. But, with our own forgetfulness of God's Divine Authority, we slipped into a personal free enterprise system governed more by man's greed. Some have called it "the robber baron era" in American History. Most of our great fortunes were amassed during this time.

Cut off from Divine authority and direction, a sense of guilt developed with the possessors of wealth and their heirs, while envy set in among the supposed "have nots," and we began to desire the stagnant security of socialism and equality.

Will Western Civilization continue to disintegrate and decay? This national nostalgia binge and rush to buy anything old shows us we are looking backward to a time which we perceive to be better. Still more to the point, the production of today does not have the quality of yesterday.

True, there is opportunity to make money, even to acquire modest incomes, but remember this: It is not particularly wonderful to be a rich man in a disintegrating society. For one thing, one must pay protection money in order to enjoy the little that is left over; even more, our homes and the lives of loved ones are not safe.

There is more to living than laying up treasure. We must also re-establish our Christian Law system and re-affirm our Faith. This must come first. Then we will be able to earn, and enjoy our future and rest in the knowledge that our heirs also will be able to carry on.

To stop the present crumbling we begin, not in Washington, D.C., but in the areas where we still have authority. As parents we still rule our homes. Reclaim as much responsibility as you can in your communities and businesses. Become leaders.

Home education, if only in the field of economics, will determine future events. Our young learn, in the home, what it is like to live in a debt-free family, or in a family environment burdened by debt. We can become wasteful or frugal according to the habits of our parents. If this present generation is content with debt living, their offspring will be ever greater borrowers than the parents. Debt living is always a progressive spiral downwards towards bankruptcy. Family money managed with proficiency and profit will bear fruit in the next generation. Teach economics in the home. This is the old "hand that rocks the cradle" theory, but that hand does not of necessity have to be, nor should it be, an exclusively feminine hand. You men should do more cradle rocking.

Next, you should insist that our schools and colleges teach and reinforce the sound money management of the family.

Begin at home, and, from this family foundation, reach out to reclaim the decision-making power and authority from the state. The rewards will be tremendous, both present and future, for our families and our nation.

# Scripture Index

# Index

147

# The Author

Rousas John Rushdoony (1916-2001) was a well-known American scholar, writer, and author of over thirty books. He held B.A. and M.A. degrees from the University of California and received his theological training at the Pacific School of Religion. An ordained minister, he worked as a missionary among Paiute and Shoshone Indians as well as a pastor to two California churches. He founded the Chalcedon Foundation, an educational organization devoted to research, publishing, and cogent communication of a distinctively Christian scholarship to the world at large. His writing in the *Chalcedon Report* and his numerous books spawned a generation of believers active in reconstructing the world to the glory of Jesus Christ. He resided in Vallecito, California until his death, where he engaged in research, lecturing, and assisting others in developing programs to put the Christian Faith into action.

# The Ministry of Chalcedon

CHALCEDON (kal•see•don) is a Christian educational organization devoted exclusively to research, publishing, and cogent communication of a distinctively Christian scholarship to the world at large. It makes available a variety of services and programs, all geared to the needs of interested ministers, scholars, and laymen who understand the propositions that Jesus Christ speaks to the mind as well as the heart, and that His claims extend beyond the narrow confines of the various institutional churches. We exist in order to support the efforts of all orthodox denominations and churches. Chalcedon derives its name from the great ecclesiastical Council of Chalcedon (A.D. 451), which produced the crucial Christological definition: "Therefore, following the holy Fathers, we all with one accord teach men to acknowledge one and the same Son, our Lord Jesus Christ, at once complete in Godhead and complete in manhood, truly God and truly man...." This formula directly challenges every false claim of divinity by any human institution: state, church, cult, school, or human assembly. Christ alone is both God and man, the unique link between heaven and earth. All human power is therefore derivative: Christ alone can announce that "All power is given unto me in heaven and in earth" (Matthew 28:18). Historically, the Chalcedonian creed is therefore the foundation of Western liberty, for it sets limits on all authoritarian human institutions by acknowledging the validity of the claims of the One who is the source of true human freedom (Galatians 5:1).

The *Chalcedon Report* is published monthly and is sent to all who request it. All gifts to Chalcedon are tax deductible.

**Chalcedon**
**Box 158**
**Vallecito, CA 95251 U.S.A.**
**www.chalcedon.edu**

2534353